EDMONDS
SURE TO RISE
PART OF NEW ZEALAND'S HERITAGE SINCE 1879

food for flatters

over 200 recipes for

small budgets,

small spaces

and big ideas

Hodder Moa

Tableware kindly supplied by

freedom

ISBN: 978-1-86958-864-9

First published in 2001 by Hodder Moa Beckett Publishers Ltd
[a member of the Hodder Headline Group],
4 Whetu Place, Mairangi Bay, Auckland, New Zealand

Reprinted 2001, 2002 (twice), 2003, 2004, 2005

Reprinted 2006 (twice), 2007, 2008, 2009, 2010, 2012
by Hachette New Zealand Ltd
4 Whetu Place, Mairangi Bay, Auckland, New Zealand

Produced and designed by Hodder Moa Beckett Publishers Ltd
Text and food styling by Sally Cameron
Photographs by Bruce Benson
Film and colour separations by Microdot, Auckland
Printed by Everbest Printing Co. Ltd, China

introduction

For most New Zealanders the name 'Edmonds' is associated with reliable ingredients that are 'sure to rise', and a cookbook that has become a virtual Kiwi icon. The first edition of the *Edmonds Cookery Book* was published over ninety years ago, and for the best part of a century Edmonds has maintained its reputation for presenting tasty, everyday recipes that are easy to prepare.

Now the Edmonds team has brought together an exciting range of recipes that are geared towards the growing number of New Zealanders that choose to go flatting. Cooking with or for flatmates can be a challenging experience and one that is guaranteed to put both the imagination and the wallet to the test. The average flatting kitchen may lack the latest utensils and equipment, the shopping list may be seriously constrained by the weekly budget, and the level of the collective cookery skills may be at the 'early development' stage. However, none of this need deter the flatter who wants to eat well every day and even impress friends and family on the odd special occasion.

Food for Flatters not only provides a wide selection of delicious ideas for meals and snacks. It also contains practical advice on how to make the most of the flatting kitchen – what basic utensils are needed, what ingredients to keep regularly in the pantry and how to organise the kitchen space to ease the pressure when preparing a meal.

It includes an easy-to-follow section on understanding food, which promises to be a much-used reference for the relative novice to cooking, and even for the more advanced chef. Ingredients, both the essential and not-so-ordinary, are explained and there are also handy suggestions of what to use when you run out of a key item.

Food for Flatters will guide you through the trickiest culinary situations and provide you with essential cooking skills – from knowing how to cook pasta and rice to perfection, to ensuring meat is always cooked just to your taste, to providing your party guests with tasty nibbles and delicacies. Scattered throughout the book are creative tips to help save time and money, boost confidence and set even the most inexperienced cook on a path to expertise in the kitchen.

Over 200 easy-to-prepare recipes in the trusted Edmonds style cater for all meals and occasions, from breakfast and brunch, snacks and salads, soups and starters to pasta and rice. The culinary tastes and dietary preferences of all flatmates are catered for in the chapters on main meals with meat, fish and shellfish and vegetarian dishes. Those flatters with a sweet tooth will really enjoy the chapters devoted to desserts and cakes and baking, while the romantics will just love the Dinner for Two chapter with its menus and recipes for creating that fabulously impressive meal for your 'special person'. A Christmas Feast and Party Food present both innovative and traditional recipes that will allow the flatting cook to impress their guests with their style and skill.

Edmonds continues to provide New Zealanders with a core repertoire of culinary skills and recipes. *Food for Flatters* is destined to become a must-have in all flatting kitchens, combining as it does fresh and funky recipes with great presentation ideas and good old-fashioned advice. We hope you enjoy cooking from this book.

The Edmonds Team, January 2001

contents

setting up
a kitchen

 A kitchen is one of the most used rooms in the house, so it should be treated as one of the most important spaces.

Perhaps you are new to flatting and starting from scratch on your own or in your first shared house. Or perhaps you're already a veteran of communal living. Whatever the case may be, there are a few things that are necessary to get you started on the path to creating beautiful cuisine.

■ Clean, efficient, safe

First things first: give your kitchen a good clean. A bottle of detergent and some elbow grease should do the trick. Clean your fridge, freezer and oven. Don't forget to clean behind the fridge and oven and any other spots where previous tenants may have failed to go for quite some time. A coat of paint (if you're allowed to paint the house) can hide a multitude of sins in a kitchen that seems beyond repair.

Organise your kitchen well. Sort out your fridge, freezer and pantry. Plan where you want things to go; think about what foods you use the most and where you are able to reach them easily. A small kitchen needn't be a drag if it is well organised.

Get rid of any junk — old toasters, old cake tins and chipped plates. Not only do they create clutter, but they are also an eyesore and can potentially pose a health risk. Double-check that all the equipment works and works well. A landlord may be unco-operative if you explain after the takeover period that the oven blew up or the cupboard door fell off. Money can also be saved if your fridge door seals properly and your oven doesn't have major temperature fluctuations. Check both oven and fridge with a thermometer before you sign a lease, and make it part of the requirements that your landlord/lady must get these appliances checked out for you.

Remember if you run your kitchen well, it can make a remarkable difference to the way you cook. Just follow the basic tips:

- clean as you go
- have a place for everything and everything in its place
- throw out what you don't need.

■ Getting equipped

To cook food you will need the right equipment. You don't need to have every trendy appliance under the sun, but it helps to have one or two of the right tools for particular jobs.

Apart from plates and cutlery, look at what else you need to cook meals for yourself and your flatmates. Cheaper equipment may be sufficient in a short-term leasehold house. There is no point in paying lots of money for items that will one day be divided between the masses or left behind.

However, it is worth spending a little extra on some items. Knives and pots, for instance, tend to be used most often. It can be a false economy to spend little and then find a repeat purchase is needed soon afterwards.

Take care of your equipment. Like anything else, the better you look after kitchen utensils, the longer they will last. Washing, fixing or oiling of all utensils, appliances and machinery may take time but will save you money in the long run.

Good storage of your equipment is essential as well. Try not to leave sharp knives in the bottom of messy cutlery drawers. Apart from the danger they represent to innocent fingers on the hunt for another device, they will also become blunt a lot more quickly if they are constantly banged about. Space-saving devices like racks and baskets help keep work surfaces clear and implements within easy reach.

The following equipment is essential for day-to-day cooking.

- **Saucepans and frying pans** — These are available in all shapes and sizes and are made of different materials. As a rule, heavy-based, stainless steel pots will be the most cost-efficient. If you don't want excess fat and oil in your cooking, Teflon-coated or non-stick pans are also an excellent option.

- **Knives** — A good-quality knife or set of knives will surpass many nifty gadgets available today. Specialist gadgets are useful, but can be expensive cupboard fillers. A good set of knives will save you time and energy and should last a lifetime. Look for a well-balanced knife that feels right when you hold it. Think about what actions (like slicing bread or cutting onions) you do the most and choose a knife suitable for the task. Choose the heaviest knife you can handle. The more weight in the metal, the less effort you have to put into cutting.

- **Chopping boards** — If you are going to use any knife and want to keep it reasonably sharp then the best advice is to use it on a decent cutting surface. Metal surfaces and Formica tops will blunt the blades. Plastic, colour-coded boards are recommended by many health authorities, but as long as you wash and dry a wooden board properly it is the best surface to cut and slice on.

- **Cooking utensils** — Wooden spoons, spatulas, tongs and whisks are all equally important. It may take you a little time to work out exactly what you need for your kitchen — usually while you are in the middle of cooking something and need the right utensil there and then! But again, get items that suit you. There's no point getting a huge whisk if you are only ever going to use it to make scrambled eggs for two.

- **Mixing bowls** — These come in varying sizes and shapes. A limited budget might mean you can only afford plastic durable bowls that double as storage containers. Advanced cooks might look to metal or glass bowls, because these make a big difference in ease of preparation.

- **Sieves, colanders, graters and peelers** — Most kitchens will have one or two of these items and they help if you are into quick cheesy pasta or potato dishes. Very inexpensive and easily obtained from supermarkets and corner stores, they are probably the equipment with the highest turnover in any kitchen.

- **Baking equipment** — You don't have to be a great patisserie chef to want to use a rolling pin or pastry brush every now and then. Cake tins, baking trays, piping bags, cutters and the like will be acquired as you become more confident with cooking skills. Amateurs and professional caterers alike will collect more baking equipment than they care to store. The same rule still applies — the better the quality, the better the job it will do for you.

- **Measuring equipment** — Not everyone can successfully measure out the right ingredients by eye. Recipes are developed using level measures so that disasters don't occur. A set of measuring spoons, cups and scales will help with your culinary experiments until you know exactly how much a 'pinch' or a 'dash' is.

- **Ovenproof dishes** — To make the all-important lasagne for the team, or to roast, bake, grill and braise just about anything, ovenproof glass or ceramic dishes are a must. Double-check that they are microwave-proof as well. Many are also dishwasher-proof and shatterproof. Pyrex is a great start. Two or three well-selected pieces will make all the difference to your preparation of meals.

- **The big stuff** — Toasters, food processors, microwaves, kettles, blenders, grinders, and so on, are the small appliances we can't seem to live without. They get bigger, better, shinier, faster and more streamlined every year. Choose wisely and your appliances will last you for much longer than the period of warranty given on the purchase card. And ask yourself one question before you hand over all that money for an automatic bread slicer or triple-action meat mincer — 'Do I really need it?' Remember, a good knife will do just as much as most of the gadgets.

- **The biggest stuff** — Fridges, freezers, ovens, dishwashers are all essentials for our modern way of living. Treat them well and they will look after you and your food. Clean them as you would clean your own teeth — regularly! Not only for hygiene reasons but also for the longevity of your investment. If you notice a fault, get it fixed straight away. Small problems can rapidly escalate to big problems. If the landlord supplies the whiteware for your rented abode, make sure they are aware of any leaks, broken racks, squeaky noises and peculiar odours as soon as possible.

■ Basic hygiene and safety

It's no good if you end up at the doctor or rushing to the bathroom every time you cook a meal. Remember to follow these basic but necessary rules of hygiene before preparing any meal.

- Wash hands thoroughly before starting to prepare food. Ensure that your work area is also clean.

- Clean chopping boards and work surfaces with hot, soapy water after cutting raw meat and between usage for cutting different foods. Raw food like meat and seafood will transfer harmful bacteria from surfaces to your mouth very easily.

- Thoroughly clean knives and other equipment that have been used for cutting raw meat or fish to prevent cross-contamination. Washing equipment also prevents the transfer of flavours like those of garlic and onions into your sweet cakes and sauces.

- Egg dishes, meats, seafood and anything that has been cooked must be refrigerated without delay once it has cooled down.

- If meat is frozen, thaw it by leaving it in the fridge overnight or by quickly defrosting it in the microwave. Try to avoid leaving it out on a bench or sink all night.

- Always reheat food thoroughly. Ensure food is brought to boiling point when reheated, not just warmed. Harmful bacteria love warm places and will grow rapidly if the conditions are right.

- Never reheat food more than once.

■ Storage

In the fridge

- **Perishable foods** such as fish, meat, poultry and dairy produce should be stored in the fridge.

- **Raw meat** should be kept separate from cooked meat and be placed at the bottom of the fridge to stop liquid from dripping onto cooked food.

- **Remove plastic wrapping** from pre-packaged foods to allow air to circulate, and cover loosely.

- **The temperature** in a fridge should be between 1ºC and 4ºC to ensure safe storage.

- **Cover food** to prevent it from drying out and to avoid the transfer of strong flavours.

- **Green and soft vegetables** should be stored in the crisper section of the fridge. Soft and short-life fruits should also be stored in the fridge.

Freezing and freezers

Before you freeze anything check that it can be frozen and that it is labelled and dated adequately. You can't refreeze food that has been frozen previously. A freezer can become a cache of forgotten foods. Freezing is still only a temporary method of storing foods, and very few foods will actually be edible after about 12 months of ice chilling.

General rules for freezing

- Do not freeze the following: cooked egg whites; stuffed poultry; custards and un-whipped creams; thickened flour sauces like white or cheese sauce; jellies; meringues; mayonnaise; salad greens like lettuce, cucumbers or spring onions.

- Divide large portions of meat, berries, vegetables, or cakes into smaller units. This will make it unnecessary to thaw all the food at once to get the amount you desire.

- Package your frozen food properly — avoid freezer burn by placing food in plastic containers and bags and eliminating as much air as possible. Glass will expand when frozen and can explode. Label and date your frozen foods for easy identification.

- Space is at a premium in the freezer and too much food in your freezer can reduce the effectiveness of the freezing thermostat. Try not to overload. Allow air to circulate around all the goods in your freezer, especially if the food item has just been put in there to chill quickly and efficiently.

- Do not put hot or boiling foods straight into the freezer. Allow them to cool down outside or in a refrigerator first. The heat will transfer from one item to another and begin the thawing process of valuable foods.

In the pantry

- **Potatoes, kumara and onions** should be stored in a cool dark place. Do not store potatoes, kumara, onions, bananas or unripe avocados in the fridge.

- **Store pantry goods** such as rice, rolled oats, dry breadcrumbs, dried fruit and flour in sealed containers. Not only will this improve their shelf life, but it will also keep insects and vermin from interfering with your precious supplies.

■ Basic store cupboard items
(what to put on the shopping list)

Your pantry will grow as you acquire food for all the yummy recipes in this book. A lot of recipes will use a full packet of important ingredients to reduce waste and to avoid the unnecessary storing of surplus goods. It is wise to buy some items when they appear on 'special', so don't be scared to purchase. You will probably use them at some stage, sooner rather than later.

Canned food and jars
red kidney beans
whole peeled tomatoes in juice
tomato purée
kernel or creamed corn
canned fruit
tuna or salmon
pasta sauce

Oils and vinegars
olive oil
soy or vegetable oil
malt vinegar

Condiments
relishes and chutneys
mustards and mustard powders
jams and honey

Sauces
soy sauce
tomato sauce
mayonnaise
Thai sweet chilli sauce
Worcestershire sauce

Baking

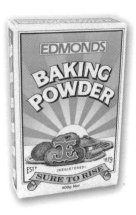

Edmonds standard grade flour

Edmonds baking powder

Edmonds baking soda

sugar, caster sugar, brown sugar

Edmonds Fielder's cornflour

Edmonds custard powder

cocoa

vanilla essence

golden syrup

Spices and herbs

salt

black peppercorns, crushed or ground

curry powder

black pepper

paprika

liquid or dry stocks

nutmeg

ground cumin

ginger

chilli powder

Pasta and noodles

macaroni elbows

spaghetti

Cereals

rolled oats

rice

dry breadcrumbs

■ Budgeting

The all-important task of watching where the cents go will help you save your dollars. You don't have to skimp on quality when living on a budget. By saving in many areas of your food and food production you can afford to spend your hard-earned money on the right things.

A few tips for saving money on your food bill

- Look out for specials and savings — if it is a product that can be stored easily, a couple of extra cans or boxes will come in handy one day. But only buy them if you know you will use them. Don't get trapped into buying food items that you don't normally consume.

- Use coupons and reward cards — these are designed to give you, the consumer, more money back on your purchases.

- Try to buy seasonally. If certain fruits and vegetables are in season, make the most of them at bargain prices. Preserve, freeze or create your own exciting recipes with produce that is good to eat now.

- Meat may look nicer if the bones have been removed or the skin taken off, but five seconds to pull the skin from a chicken breast yourself may be all you need to save yourself a little extra cash.

- Support your local butcher rather than purchasing meat from the supermarket. You will save money and be able to buy the exact quantities and cuts that you need.

- Create new and exciting dishes with leftovers. Providing you take care when reheating food, yesterday's dinner may be a delightful lunch or re-hashed meal.

- Check 'best before' dates when you buy perishable foods. A carton of milk with one day to go will be wasted if you aren't gong to consume it rapidly.

- Shop around — convenience shopping can create complacency and may mean you lose out on cost competition.

understanding food

■ Herbs

Herbs are varied and plentiful and do make a world of difference to your cooking. They offer a range of flavours: grassy, peppery, aromatic or pungent. They will enhance your sauces, casseroles or salads with very little effort on your part.

Growing your own herbs is a therapeutic and cost-effective way of always having a fresh supply. Failing this, use fresh herbs grown in hydroponic pots, or substitute dried herbs. As a general rule, allow one-third tablespoon of dried herbs to every one tablespoon of fresh. Dried herbs do lose their flavour with age and can become stale. Try to keep dried herbs in airtight containers and replace them as often as you can.

There are plenty of dried herbs available and knowing what to use them for can be as simple as reading the packet. However, as a rule of thumb, the following herbs, whether fresh or dried, are good in the following dishes:

Basil — Most commonly available is sweet basil. It has a rich, peppery flavour and a powerful aroma. Used in Mediterranean and Italian dishes, basil is best fresh. When cut, basil will lose its green colour quickly, so use it promptly.

Bay leaves — Usually added during the cooking process, then removed just before serving the dish. Ideally suited to meats such as beef and lamb, and used most commonly in slow-cooked soups, casseroles and stews.

Coriander — This is a powerful herb and is most common in Indian, Asian and South American cooking. It looks like parsley, but will give a lot of zing to guacamole or salsa.

Chives — These give a delicate onion flavour to any dish. Sprinkle on baked potatoes or egg dishes.

Dill — Has a delicate flavour and accompanies seafood or salmon perfectly. Can also be used with boiled potatoes and cream-cheese-based dishes.

Sage — Has a strong, dominant flavour. It goes well with pork or chicken and usually has to be cooked well in any dish.

Parsley — There are two types of parsley, curly and flat or Italian. Parsley goes well in Middle-Eastern dishes but will provide colour and grassy flavours to almost any dish. It is the most inexpensive and easily grown of all herbs.

Oregano — Used commonly in Italian cuisine, oregano flavours tomato dishes such as pasta sauce, pizza or bolognese.

Marjoram — A sweeter version of oregano ideal for Mediterranean food such as pizzas and tomato sauces.

Mint — Another frequently used herb, it is very hardy and grows well in the garden. New potatoes taste divine when boiled with mint, or use mint as an accompaniment to lamb dishes.

Rosemary — This has a pronounced flavour and tends to be very indigestible. Great flavour for beef and lamb dishes.

Tarragon — Fresh tarragon is sweet and spicy. Excellent when used to prepare chicken, egg or fish dishes. If growing your own, look for French, not Russian, tarragon.

■ Spices

Remember that if you leave spices in the pantry for too long they will lose their flavour and pungency. As a rule, spices should be kept for no longer than three months.

Commonly used spices

Cardamom — Highly aromatic seeds that are used a lot in curries and to perfume coffee.

Cayenne — A type of ground pepper. Cayenne is very hot and a small amount can give a lot of flavour to a dish.

Chilli powder — The ground-up flesh and seeds of the chilli. Very spicy and puts heat into any recipe.

Cinnamon — The inner bark of a type of evergreen tree. It is sold in quills or as a powder and can be used in both sweet and savoury dishes.

Coriander powder — The ground-up seeds from the coriander plant, often used in curries. The fresh leaves are a popular herb.

Cumin — This is a delicate and mild spice and teams up well with coriander. Often used in Mexican and Middle-Eastern cooking.

Mixed spice — A mixture of nutmeg, cinnamon and coriander.

Nutmeg — Good to buy whole as a nut and to grate into dishes, but normally bought ground. Best used in cheesy sauces and vegetable dishes.

Paprika — The ground powder of a pepper. Not as hot as normal, it can be either smoky or sweet in flavour.

Star anise — This spice has a flavour half-way between aniseed and liquorice. It is an essential ingredient of Chinese five spice powder.

Turmeric — Usually sold ground, this is perhaps the easiest spice to recognise, because of its bright yellow colour. Often used as a cheap substitute for saffron, but can be quite bitter.

■ Cheese and dairy products

Fresh cheeses

Cream cheese — A soft cheese made principally from cream.

Mascarpone — An Italian cheese made by adding tartaric acid to natural cheese curds. Used in the popular Tiramisu and other Italian desserts. Also popular in savoury foods.

Mozzarella — A cheese made from cows' milk, usually sold with a milky whey. It has a mild flavour and melts well.

Ricotta — A cottage-cheese-like product made from curds.

Semi-soft cheeses

Edam — A cheese named after a port in Amsterdam, principally sold coated in red wax.

Gouda — A Dutch cheese that is firm and smooth with a sweet nutty flavour. Comes in a wax or plastic rind.

Soft white cheeses

Brie and camembert — Named after the regions in France where they were originally produced. These cheeses are ripened from the inside, leaving a white mould rind on the outside.

Blue cheeses

Blue vein and bleu de bresse — Blue mould is added to the milk, then metal rods are used to pierce the cheese, allowing air to enter and thus encourage the mould to grow.

Hard cheeses

Cheddar — The most common hard cheese. It comes in a range from mild, tasty to mature, depending on how long the cheese has been kept.

Parmesan — A cheese made from cows' milk, usually matured for between nine and 12 years before being used. Its strong flavour means only a little is needed in any dish.

Pecorino — A goats' milk cheese made in a similar way to parmesan.

Cream-based products

Crème fraîche — Usually a blend of sour cream and cream with 35% to 48% milk fat. It is less tart than sour cream and is great for thickening soups and sauces.

Sour cream — A culture is added to milk to produce a tart flavour. Used in dips, sauces, cakes and Mexican dishes.

■ Flours, rising agents and grains

It is important to use the right flour or grain as specified in a recipe. Each flour has its very own characteristics that make it behave the way it does when it is cooked.

Edmonds standard grade flour — This is ideal for most cakes, baking and sauces. Standard flour has a lower protein (gluten) content which helps make baked products soft and tender.

Edmonds high grade flour — This has a high protein (gluten) content, which is important in bread making to ensure that the dough, when kneaded, has sufficient strength to give the bread good volume and texture.

Edmonds self-raising flour — This is a blend of standard grade flour and rising ingredients. Self-raising flour can replace the flour and baking powder in recipes for scones, muffins, pikelets, pancakes and many cakes and slices.

Edmonds wholemeal flour — This is made from all parts of the wheat grain: the white flour, bran and wheatgerm. Wholemeal flour contains more fibre than white flour and adds a nutty flavour to muffins, bread, pie-crusts, crumbles and fruit loaves.

Edmonds baking powder — Baking powder is a mixture of cream of tartar and baking soda plus wheat flour. It helps leaven baking and therefore helps cakes and baked goods rise.

Edmonds baking soda — Baking soda is also known as bicarbonate of soda.

Edmonds Fielder's cornflour — This is made from maize and is a starch used to thicken products such as sauces and desserts, or it can be used in baked products.

Rolled oats — An important source of nutrients supplying carbohydrates, protein and vitamins. Great for breakfast, in stuffings and in baking muffins and biscuits.

Wheatgerm flakes — These are high in natural fibre and contain other nutrients to help balance your diet. Sprinkle on fruit and cereal or add to muffins, muesli or biscuits.

■ Cooking terms

Al dente — Used to describe cooked pasta that is firm to the bite and ready to eat.

Baking blind — Baking a pastry case before the filling is added. Loosely cover an unbaked pastry case with a sheet of baking paper larger than the size of the tin. Fill with dried beans or rice and bake. You can store the beans or rice and reuse them next time for baking blind.

Baking paper — Suitable for lining cake tins and trays. Does not need to be greased, although it may need a smear of butter to make it adhere to the tin.

Baste — To spoon juices over foods being roasted in order to prevent drying and to give a glossy surface.

Blanch — To place fruit and vegetables in boiling water for 30 seconds and then in cold water. This makes it easy to remove skins (e.g. of tomatoes) or is done to prepare the food for freezing.

Blend — To mix ingredients thoroughly in order to get an even consistency.

Boil — To cook in water at boiling point with large rolling bubbles forming.

Bouquet garni — A selection of herbs, usually fresh, tied together with string or in muslin. A bouquet garni always includes sprigs of thyme and parsley and a bay leaf. Used to flavour soups and stews. Should be removed once cooking is complete.

Cream — To beat softened butter with sugar until light, fluffy and creamy in colour.

Fold — To combine a delicate mixture with a heavier one by using a metal spoon in a cutting action, cutting down through the centre and bringing the bottom mixture to the top. Used for additions of whipped cream and beaten egg whites.

Frothy — Describes a mixture at stage when it is full of small bubbles. When making white sauce, heat butter and flour until mixture appears frothy with small bubbles before adding liquid.

Knead — To press non-yeast doughs together quickly in order to combine — e.g. pastry, biscuits and scone doughs. To stretch and fold yeast doughs repeatedly in order to develop elasticity.

Marinate — To leave meat, poultry or fish in a tenderising or flavouring liquid (the marinade) for a period of time.

Mash — To crush food until soft. This can be done with a fork or potato masher.

Pan grill — To heat a dry, heavy-based frying pan until very hot before oiled meat is put in.

Purée — To mash or sieve cooked fruit or vegetables to give a smooth, semi-liquid result.

Sauté — To fry foods in a small amount of hot oil quickly, shaking and stirring the pan to get even cooking.

Sieve — To press or shake through a mesh to get an even consistency.

Sift — To shake dry ingredients through a mesh to remove lumps or foreign matter, or to mix evenly.

Simmer — To cook just at boiling point, not at a full rolling boil.

Skim — To remove fat or scum from the surface of a liquid with a slotted spoon, an ordinary spoon or using absorbent paper.

Stir-fry — To stir and toss prepared ingredients in hot oil very quickly. This cooking method results in moist meats and crisp vegetables.

Stiffly beaten egg whites — Egg whites beaten until peaks that are formed hold their shape, but the tips bend over. The mixture should be glossy.

Zest — Finely sliced or grated peel of an orange, lemon or lime, used for flavouring.

understanding
food

Some not-so-ordinary ingredients

Balsamic vinegar — A thick, dark, Italian vinegar, with a sweet-and-sour flavour. Traditionally matured in oak, balsamic vinegar is expensive, but an excellent investment — a little bit goes a long way.

Burghul wheat — A milled grain, that is soaked and used in salads and soups.

Buttermilk — A tangy product made by adding a bacterial culture to low-fat milk.

Chow chow relish — A preserve traditionally made from cauliflower, green tomatoes, gherkins and spices.

Coconut cream (or coconut milk) — Available canned or powdered, or can be made by mixing 1¼ cups of coconut with 300 ml of boiling water, then straining through a sieve and reserving the liquid. This will give about 1 cup (250 ml) of coconut milk.

Couscous — A type of tiny pasta made from rolling a dough to make granules. Used mostly in salads and Moroccan food.

Filo pastry — Tissue-paper-thin pastry, traditionally used for strudels. It can be bought in packets from the chiller and once opened should be used within a week or 10 days. When working with filo pastry (sometimes written as 'phyllo') place it under a damp tea towel to prevent it from drying out and becoming brittle and hard to manage.

Fish sauce — Made by fermenting small fish or shrimps. It is very pungent but gives a delicate fish flavour to Asian dishes.

Hoisin sauce — A thick, flavoured sauce, used in Asian cooking to marinate chicken or seafood. Usually made from soy sauce, oyster sauce, tomato purée and Chinese five spice, it is tangy and rich and a little goes a long way.

Jalapeño peppers — These are peppers that come in a variety of degrees of hotness and that are widely used in Mexican cooking. They are available canned or in jars from the supermarket.

Kremelta — This is not used very often in cooking nowadays. Kremelta is made from coconut oil. It is hard and can be melted down for sweets and baking.

Miso — A seasoning paste made from fermented grains, usually rice or barley and soybeans. Used most commonly in Asian food such as Japanese Miso Soup.

Naan bread — A leavened bread made with yoghurt and yeast. Traditional with Indian cuisine.

Oyster sauce — A fermented sauce made from oysters. Stronger in flavour and very rich, it is used in small amounts in Asian cooking.

Pickled ginger — Thinly sliced pieces of ginger marinated in a salty syrup. Popular in Japanese-style cooking and available from Asian supermarkets.

Rice noodles — These come in many widths, so choose a thin one nearest in size to vermicelli. Fresh rice noodles (you will find them in packets of 400 g or 450 g) are available in some oriental stores, but only keep for one or two days in the fridge. If rice noodles are unavailable, use fine egg noodles.

Sambal oelek — A paste made from hot chillies and salt.

Semolina — Flour milled from durum wheat, used in pasta or other doughs.

Soy milk — Made by grinding soy beans and mixing with water. Used as a substitute for dairy milk.

Tahini — This is a paste made from toasted sesame seeds, and it is widely used in Middle-Eastern cooking. It has a toasted nut flavour, and is often an ingredient in hummus.

Tofu — The coagulated curds from soy milk. Pressed into a block, it provides natural protein and is used in many vegetarian dishes.

■ Ingredient substitutes

If you find you have run out of a particular ingredient, don't despair — there are a few things that can be used as substitutes to make your cooking work a treat.

Fresh tomatoes — canned tomatoes
Always keep canned tomatoes on hand. They can be used in many sauces, such as pasta sauce or bolognese sauce. Canned tomatoes may also be puréed to make an easy soup (see page 58).

Fresh breadcrumbs — dried breadcrumbs
Fresh breadcrumbs provide a crisp and full outer crumb, but dried crumbs can easily be substituted and have the benefit of lasting well if stored in an airtight container. To make your own fresh breadcrumbs, trim the crusts from any fresh or stale bread. Process in a blender or food processor, or use a grater to finely shred the bread.

Olive oil — vegetable oil
Olive oil is the juice that comes from pressing olives. Extra virgin olive oil is the name given to the first press; light olive oil comes from subsequent presses. Olive oil is used primarily in dressings and vinaigrettes. To cook with it, take care not to over-heat it as it will smoke at a lower temperature than many other oils. Vegetable oil normally comes from natural seeds and soy beans. It has a higher cooking temperature and so can be used for deep frying and high-heat cooking.

Tomato purée — tomato sauce
Tomato purée is a thick blend of tomatoes, reduced until much of the moisture has evaporated. It is the basis of many tomato products, including tomato sauce. The concentrated form can be used to intensify pasta sauces and chilli dishes. Tomato sauce contains more sugar and so makes an ideal ingredient for marinades.

Beef stock — coffee
If you are making a lamb or beef recipe that needs beef stock but you don't have any, use a little black coffee instead. The flavour of coffee complements lamb surprisingly well.

Sugar — honey
Sugar is sweeter than honey and substituting brown sugar for white sugar will give a different flavour and colour to food. Honey provides a more earthy sweetness, and is ideal for flavouring drinks and marinades.

■ Handy sauces and marinades

White Sauce
2 tablespoons butter
2 tablespoons Edmonds standard grade flour
1 cup milk
salt
pepper

Melt butter in a small saucepan. Add flour and stir constantly for 2 minutes. Remove from heat. Gradually add milk, stirring constantly, then return to heat and stir until sauce thickens and comes to the boil. Season with salt and pepper to taste.

MAKES 1 CUP

Cheese Sauce
After cooking White Sauce above, remove pan from heat. Stir in 1/2 cup grated tasty cheddar cheese.

MAKES 1 CUP

Microwave Cheese Sauce
2 tablespoons butter
2 tablespoons Edmonds standard grade flour
pepper
1 cup milk
1/2 cup grated tasty cheddar cheese

Place butter in 2-cup capacity microwave-proof jug. Cover and heat on High (100%) for 40–50 seconds to melt. Stir in flour and pepper, then add milk and stir thoroughly to blend. Cook on High for 3–3 1/2 minutes, stirring twice, until sauce is thick and smooth. Stir in cheese.

MAKES ABOUT 1 1/2 CUPS

Curry Sauce
In the White Sauce recipe above, include 1–2 teaspoons curry powder when adding flour.

MAKES 1 CUP

Onion Sauce
Add 1 sliced onion to butter in the White Sauce recipe and cook until soft. Continue as above.

MAKES 1 CUP

Parsley Sauce

2 tablespoons butter
2 tablespoons Edmonds standard grade flour
1 cup milk
$^1/_2$ cup chicken stock
$^1/_2$ teaspoon salt
1 egg yolk
5 tablespoons sour cream
2–3 tablespoons finely chopped parsley

Place butter in a 4-cup capacity microwave-proof jug or bowl. Cover with a paper towel and heat on High (100%) for 40–45 seconds to melt. Stir in flour until blended. Gradually add milk and stock, stirring continuously until smooth. Cook on High for 3$^1/_2$–4 minutes, stirring twice, until sauce boils and thickens. Beat in salt, egg yolk, sour cream and parsley. Heat on High for 35–40 seconds. Do not boil. Serve with fish and egg dishes. **MAKES ABOUT 2 CUPS**

Hollandaise Sauce

2 tablespoons butter
1 tablespoon lemon juice
2 egg yolks
$^1/_4$ cup cream
$^1/_2$ teaspoon dry mustard
$^1/_4$ teaspoon salt

Melt the butter in a bowl placed over a saucepan of simmering water. Add lemon juice, egg yolks and cream. Cook, stirring constantly, until thick and smooth. Do not boil, or sauce will curdle. Remove from heat. Add mustard and salt and beat until smooth. **MAKES $^3/_4$ CUP**

Spicy Barbecue Sauce

1 cup tomato sauce
$^1/_2$ cup water
3 tablespoons golden syrup
$^1/_2$ teaspoon salt
2 teaspoons Worcestershire sauce
$^1/_2$ teaspoon curry powder
freshly ground black pepper
1 clove garlic, crushed
$^1/_4$ cup dry red wine

Combine all ingredients. Leave to stand for 5–6 hours. **MAKES 2 CUPS**

Barbecue Marinade

2 tablespoons tomato sauce
1 teaspoon sugar
1 tablespoon soy sauce
$^1/_4$ cup chilli sauce
2 cloves garlic, crushed

Combine all ingredients in a bowl. Mix well. Place meat in mixture, coating well. Cover and leave to marinate for at least 1 hour. Suitable for steaks, chicken, lamb and pork.

Spicy Marinade

$^3/_4$ cup coconut milk
3 tablespoons soy sauce
3 tablespoons vegetable oil
3 cloves garlic, crushed
1 teaspoon ground cumin
1 teaspoon ground coriander

Combine all ingredients in a bowl. Place meat in mixture. Cover and refrigerate for 1–2 hours. Suitable for steak, chicken and shelled prawns.

■ Barbecue tips

Barbecues are a great New Zealand tradition and provide an excellent excuse to cook outside.

- Set up a barbecue in a safe area, away from wooden houses or wood piles. Usually made from bricks or metal trays, a barbecue can be fashioned out of anything that will hold the heat source and provide an even, flat cooking surface.

- To make a small impromptu barbecue, use an old biscuit tin. Punch holes around the side of the tin. Fill the tin with charcoal or small pieces of hardwood and light. Place a metal rack or grill plate on the top. Leave to heat up sufficiently in an open space.

- Before you begin your barbecue, clean the grate or grill plate well. Use foil to line old barbecue plates to avoid food sticking to them. Choose hardwoods or charcoal for longer-lasting embers and even cooking. If using gas, check that the gas bottle is filled before you start.

- Wait for the grill plate to heat up properly before cooking anything. Allow charcoal to burn for at least 25–30 minutes. Gas barbecues should take between 10 and 15 minutes to heat up sufficiently.

- It may help to pre-cook meats and vegetables before putting them on a barbecue. This will reduce the charring that would occur if they were cooked properly all the way through on the barbecue.

- Not only meat can be cooked on the barbecue. Try slicing vegetables thinly, brushing the slices with oil and laying them on a flat grill plate. Fruit kebabs (page 115) or pieces of cake can be grilled for easy summer desserts. Bread can be wrapped in tinfoil and heated through on top or in the embers of a barbecue.

- Sear meats by flash-frying them on the hottest part of the barbecue before moving them to the side of the plate to continue cooking. This will prevent moisture loss and over-charring of the meat.

- Always let the meat rest (or stand) before serving. This will help the muscles of the meat relax after the cooking process and the meat will therefore be more palatable.

Note: It's a good idea always to have a garden hose or tap near your barbecue cooking area — just in case you need to douse the fire in a hurry!

■ Roasting or grilling meat

Roasting meat at 160ºC to 180ºC

Meat	Minutes per 500 g
Beef	
rare	20–30
medium	25–35
well done	40–45
Chicken	
Must be cooked until	
juices run clear	30
Lamb	
medium rare	20–30
medium	25–30
well done	35–40
Pork	
medium	25–35
well done	40–45
Veal	
well done	35–40

Approximate grilling times for meat

Grilling times depend on the thickness of the meat and its temperature immediately before cooking. Ideally, meat should be at room temperature before it is grilled.

Beef steaks (2–2.5cm thick)
rare	3–4 minutes each side
medium	5–6 minutes each side
well done	6 minutes each side, then reduce heat and cook to your liking

Chicken
Chicken wings and nibbles	6–9 minutes each side
Chicken breasts and legs	8–10 minutes each side

Lamb chops and cutlets
medium	5–6 minutes each side
well done	7–8 minutes each side

Pork steaks and chops
medium	4–6 minutes each side
well done	7–8 minutes each side

■ Weights and measures

New Zealand Standard metric cup and spoon measures are used in all recipes.
All measurements are level.

Easy measuring — Use measuring cups or jugs for liquid measures and sets of
1 cup, 1/2 cup, 1/3 cup and 1/4 cup for dry ingredients.

Brown sugar measurements — Are firmly packed so that the sugar will hold the
shape of the cup when tipped out.

Eggs — No. 6 eggs are used as the standard size.

Abbreviations

l = litre
ml = millilitre
cm = centimetre
mm = millimetre
g = gram
kg = kilogram
ºC = degrees Celsius

Standard measures

1 cup = 250 millilitres
1 litre = 4 cups
1 tablespoon = 15 millilitres
1 dessertspoon = 10 millilitres
1 teaspoon = 5 millilitres
1/2 teaspoon = 2.5 millilitres
1/4 teaspoon = 1.25 millilitres

Approximate metric/imperial conversions

Weight
25 g = 1 ounce
125 g = 4 ounces
225 g = 8 ounces
500 g = 1 pound
1 kg = 2 1/4 pounds

Volume
1 litre = 1 3/4 pints

Measurements
1 cm = 1/2 inch
20 cm = 8 inches
30 cm = 12 inches

Weights and measures — approximate equivalents

Item	Measure	Weight
breadcrumbs (fresh)	1 cup	50 g
butter	2 tablespoons	30 g
cheese (grated, firmly packed)	1 cup	100 g
cocoa	4 tablespoons	25 g
coconut	1 cup	75 g
cornflour	4 tablespoons	25 g
cream	1/2 pint	300 ml
dried fruit (currants, sultanas, raisins, dates)	1 cup	150–175 g
flour	1 cup	125 g
golden syrup	1 tablespoon	25 g
milk	1 cup	250 ml
oil	1 tablespoon	15 ml
rice, sago	2 tablespoons	25 g
	1 cup	200 g
salt	2 tablespoons	25 g
sugar, white	2 tablespoons	30 g
	1 cup	250 g
sugar, brown	1 cup (firmly packed)	200 g
	1 cup (loosely packed)	125–150 g
sugar, icing	1 cup	150 g
standard No. 6 egg		about 50 g

Before and after equivalent measures
Approximate amounts needed to give measures:
1/3 cup uncooked rice = 1 cup cooked rice
1/3 cup uncooked pasta = 1 cup cooked pasta
2–3 chicken pieces = 1 cup cooked chicken
100 g cheese = 1 cup grated cheese
75 g mushrooms = 1 cup sliced = 1/2 cup cooked
4 toast slices bread = 1 cup fresh breadcrumbs
200 g (two) potatoes = 1 cup mashed potato

■ Oven know-how

Oven conversions
160ºC = 325ºF
180ºC = 350ºF
190ºC = 375ºF
200ºC = 400ºF

A guide to oven temperatures and use

Product	ºC	ºF	Gas No.	Description
meringues, pavlova	110–140	225–175	1/4–1	slow
custards, milk puddings, shortbread, rich fruit cakes, casseroles, slow roasting	150–160	300–325	2–3	moderately slow
biscuits, large and small cakes	180–190	350–375	4–5	moderate
roasting, sponges, muffins, short pastry	190–220	375–425	5–6	moderately hot
flaky pastry, scones, browning toppings	220–230	425–450	6–8	hot
puff pastry	250–260	475–500	9–10	very hot

Oven hints
Cooking temperatures and times given in this book are a guide only as ovens may vary. Always preheat oven to required temperature before food preparation.

Oven racks — position before turning oven on.

Oven positions
> *Bottom of oven* — use for slow cooking and low temperature cooking
> *Middle of oven* — for moderate temperature cooking
> *Above middle* — for quick cooking and high temperature cooking

Fan-forced ovens — refer to the manufacturer's directions as the models vary.

breakfast
and brunch

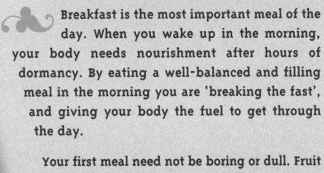

Breakfast is the most important meal of the day. When you wake up in the morning, your body needs nourishment after hours of dormancy. By eating a well-balanced and filling meal in the morning you are 'breaking the fast', and giving your body the fuel to get through the day.

Your first meal need not be boring or dull. Fruit is an exceptional start, giving you natural sugars and fibre. For the more indulgent, a satisfying start is provided by eggs — which are a great protein boost.

For those on the run, breakfast doesn't have to be a chore. Make it something to look forward to in the morning — a reason to get up and out of bed.

Brunch is a great excuse to be more creative and to enjoy preparing yourself a meal. An egg is a good way to start. A hen's egg white consists of almost 100% protein, so you can't go wrong. Don't be scared of the egg; it is an easy way to start your cooking lessons and makes a flavoursome meal in minutes.

Omelettes can be flavoured with an array of goodies like ham, cheese or mushrooms; or be more adventurous and try tuna, smoked fish, spicy sausage or a mixture of field and brown mushrooms. Cereals don't need to be limited to nuts and grains. Mix dried apricots, figs or dried tropical fruits in with your rolled oats to make a tasty muesli.

Breakfast can be turned into a social occasion instead of a chore first thing in the morning. Take the time and breakfast like a king or queen.

fruit smoothie

¹/₄ of a whole pineapple
1 whole banana, skin removed
3–4 strawberries, hulled

¹/₂ orange, skin removed
¹/₂ cup blueberries, fresh or frozen
2 cups ice cubes

Place fruit and ice cubes in a blender or food processor. Blend for 30 seconds until well puréed. Serve immediately.   **SERVES 4**

toasted muesli

¹/₄ cup oil
¹/₄ cup brown sugar
¹/₄ cup honey
3 cups rolled oats
¹/₂ cup coconut
¹/₂ cup wheatgerm flakes

¹/₂ cup bran flakes
¹/₂ cup sesame seeds
¹/₂ cup sunflower seeds
¹/₂ cup chopped nuts
¹/₂ to 1 cup raisins or sultanas

Put oil, sugar and honey into a saucepan. Heat gently until sugar dissolves. In a bowl, combine rolled oats, coconut, wheatgerm, bran flakes, sesame and sunflower seeds and nuts. Pour oil mixture over and mix thoroughly. Turn into a large roasting pan. Bake at 150ºC for 30–40 minutes or until lightly browned. Stir occasionally. Leave to cool. Add raisins or sultanas. Store in an airtight container.

MAKES ABOUT 6 CUPS

fresh and fruity

Make dried fruit juicy and plump again by leaving to soak overnight in a little water. Dried apricots, peaches, pineapple etc. can all then be used in fruit smoothies, porridge and pancakes or as a topping on your cereal or ice-cream.

fruity porridge

2 cups rolled oats
1 cup dried apricots
1 cup sultanas
567 g can sliced apple

1 teaspoon salt
4 cups hot water
$^1/_4$ cup maple syrup
cream, to serve

❧ Mix all ingredients except maple syrup and cream in a large saucepan. Bring to the boil, then reduce heat and cook for 15–20 minutes until oats have thickened. Add maple syrup and serve with cream. **SERVES 4**

pancakes

1 cup Edmonds standard grade
   flour
$^1/_8$ teaspoon salt
1 egg

$^3/_4$ cup milk
water

❧ Sift flour and salt into a bowl. Add egg, mixing to combine. Gradually beat in milk, mixing to a smooth batter. Chill for 1 hour. Stir. The batter will thicken on standing. Add a little water if necessary to bring it back to the original consistency. Heat a greased pancake pan or small frying pan. Pour in just enough batter to cover base of pan. Cook until golden on underside. Release with knife around edges. Flip or turn and cook other side. Stack pancakes as you cook. Serve sprinkled with lemon juice and sugar. **SERVES 4**

stodge buster

Always allow the pancake batter to stand for up to one hour before cooking. This makes the starch in the flour soften and therefore results in lighter, less stodgy pancakes.

fluffy fruit **pancakes**

2 cups Edmonds standard grade
   flour
50 g sugar
1 teaspoon Edmonds baking
   powder
1/2 teaspoon Edmonds baking soda
1/4 teaspoon salt

1 cup milk
2 eggs, separated
zest of 1 lemon
5 tablespoons butter
120 g fresh or frozen blueberries
maple syrup or honey, to serve
whipped cream, to serve

꙰ Preheat a heavy-based frying pan or grill plate. Sift flour, sugar, baking powder, baking soda and salt into a large bowl.

In another bowl, whisk milk, egg yolks and lemon zest. Melt 2 tablespoons of butter and add to bowl. Pour wet ingredients into dry ingredients and gently whisk until just combined.

Beat egg whites until peaks are stiff but not dry. Fold into batter.

Gently fold in blueberries. Melt a little of the remaining butter in frying pan or on grill plate. Spoon 2 tablespoons of batter per pancake into heated frying pan or onto grill plate, forming several rounds. Cook until pancakes are speckled with bubbles and some bubbles have popped. Turn. Cook until lightly browned. Keep warm while you cook the rest. Serve with maple syrup or honey and whipped cream. **SERVES 6**

eggy bread

1 loaf of unsliced bread
6 tablespoons olive oil
8 eggs

salt and freshly ground
   black pepper
1 cup grated tasty cheddar cheese
1 teaspoon wholegrain mustard

꙰ Preheat grill. Remove crusts then cut bread into 8 thick slices. Cut a circle from the centre of each slice using a 7.5-cm-diameter cutter or the rim of a glass.

Heat olive oil in a frying pan. Fry bread slices on one side, 3 or 4 at a time. Crack an egg into each circle. Season to taste with salt and pepper. Cook for 5 minutes, until egg is just set.

Mix grated cheese with mustard. Sprinkle over eggs. Cook under a medium grill for 2 minutes until cheese begins to melt. Serve immediately. **SERVES 4**

french **toast**

2 eggs
2 tablespoons milk
salt and freshly ground
  black pepper

4–6 slices toast bread
butter

ℒ Lightly beat eggs and milk together. Season with salt and pepper to taste. Cut slices of bread in half. Heat butter in a frying pan. Dip bread in egg.

Place in frying pan and cook until golden on underside. Turn and cook the other side. Omit salt and pepper for sweet French toast. **SERVES 4**

mousetraps

4 slices toast bread
1 cup grated tasty cheddar cheese
1 onion, finely chopped
2 tablespoons chutney

salt and freshly ground
  black pepper
chopped parsley

ℒ Toast the bread on one side only. Combine cheese and onion. Spread un-toasted side of bread with chutney. Top with cheese mixture. Season with salt and pepper to taste. Place mousetraps on an oven tray. Grill until golden. Garnish with chopped parsley. **SERVES 2–4**

eggs-actly

As a rule, there is no difference between a white or brown egg. Keep eggs refrigerated and before using check 'best before' date on the packaging. Bring to room temperature before cooking.

scrambled **egg**

1 egg
1 tablespoon milk
salt and freshly ground
    black pepper

1 teaspoon butter
1 tablespoon chopped parsley
1 slice buttered toast

Lightly beat egg. Add milk, salt and pepper to taste. Melt butter in a small frying pan. Pour in egg mixture and cook over a low heat until set. Using a wooden spoon, carefully drag the mixture from the outside edge of the pan to the centre to allow the mixture to cook evenly. Scrambled eggs should have large clots of cooked egg, so do not stir vigorously. Stir in parsley and serve on hot buttered toast. If egg is overcooked, it will become tough with a watery liquid separating out.

SERVES 1

Variations
*   Add finely sliced mushrooms to uncooked egg mixture.
*   Fold cooked, chopped bacon in after eggs are cooked.
*   Fold chopped smoked salmon in after eggs are cooked.

---

eggs benedict

3 English muffins
1 tablespoon butter
6 slices ham
6 eggs
1 teaspoon white vinegar

salt and freshly ground
    black pepper
1/2 cup Hollandaise Sauce
    (see page 28)

Split the muffins and toast them. Keep them warm. Melt the butter in a frying pan. Add ham and cook until golden on both sides.

While ham is cooking, poach the eggs. Half to three-quarters fill a frying pan with water. Add the vinegar and bring to the boil. Break the eggs into the water. Turn down the heat and simmer gently until white is just set.

Place a slice of ham on each muffin. Place poached eggs on top of ham. Season with salt and pepper to taste. Top with Hollandaise Sauce.

SERVES 6

omelette

2 eggs
1 tablespoon milk
salt and freshly ground
    black pepper

2 teaspoons butter
parsley

Lightly beat egg and milk together. Season with salt and pepper to taste. Heat an omelette pan. Add the butter. When butter is foaming, but not brown, pour in the egg mixture. Cook over moderate heat, lifting mixture at the outside edge of the pan with a spatula so uncooked egg runs underneath.

Cook until egg is set and golden. Loosen from pan with spatula. Fold in half. Turn out onto a hot serving dish. Garnish with parsley.   **SERVES 1**

bacon and egg salad

200 g cooked shoulder bacon,
    diced
2 eggs, hard-boiled and chopped
1 cup diced celery
2 spring onions, chopped
3 tablespoons mayonnaise
1 teaspoon lemon juice

1 teaspoon Dijon mustard
a pinch of pepper
2 cups mesclun leaves
4 cherry tomatoes, halved

Combine all ingredients except mesclun and tomatoes in a large bowl. Cover and refrigerate until chilled.

Arrange mesclun on a platter. Spoon bacon mixture on top and surround with cherry tomatoes.   **SERVES 2**

eggs-pulsion

When boiling an egg, make a pin prick in the rounded end of the raw egg. This will allow steam to escape and therefore the eggshell will not crack.

ham and vegetable frittata

2 tablespoons oil
1 onion, finely chopped
1 cup small broccoli florets
2 cloves garlic, crushed
1 tablespoon Dijon mustard
8 eggs
salt and freshly ground
    black pepper

2 cups diced cooked potatoes
    (about 2 large potatoes)
4 slices ham, diced
1¹/₂ cups grated tasty
    cheddar cheese

Heat oil in a heavy-based, 25-cm frying pan with a heatproof handle. Cook onion, broccoli, garlic and mustard over a medium heat for 5 minutes. Lightly beat eggs and salt and pepper. Add potatoes and ham to pan, stirring to combine.

Spread mixture evenly over base of pan. Reduce heat to low. Pour eggs evenly over vegetable mixture. Sprinkle with cheese. Cook for about 8 minutes until frittata is half cooked. Meanwhile, preheat oven grill.

Place frittata under grill for 3–4 minutes until set and golden. Leave in pan for 5 minutes before cutting into wedges. Serve either warm or cold. **SERVES 4**

hash brown potatoes

500 g potatoes, peeled and
    chopped
¹/₂ teaspoon salt

50 g butter
2 rashers bacon, finely chopped
1 tablespoon chopped chives

Cook potatoes in boiling, salted water until tender. Drain well then leave to cool. Mash. Melt butter in a large frying pan. Add bacon and cook until crisp. Using a slotted spoon, remove bacon from pan. Do not discard fat.

Spread potato over base of frying pan. Press down until even. Cook over a low heat for 25 minutes or until underside is a deep golden brown. Turn, using a spatula, and cook other side. Scoop potato out of pan and into heated serving dish. Sprinkle with bacon and chives. **SERVES 4**

snacks

To snack or not to snack? Sometimes when hunger grabs you there is no option but to reach for something substantial to tide you over until your next meal. Making snacks healthy, quick to prepare and exciting is the next big hurdle.

Breads help fill the gap for hungry tums, and having a supply in the freezer solves the problem of having to dash out to buy some. Pita bread and crostini can be kept on hand so that you can snack-and-go.

For the more substantial hunger pangs, baked potatoes are nutritious and everyone's favourites. And when the crowds come round and you want something to keep them going, serve simple cheeseboards and antipasto platters to tempt tastebuds with new flavours.

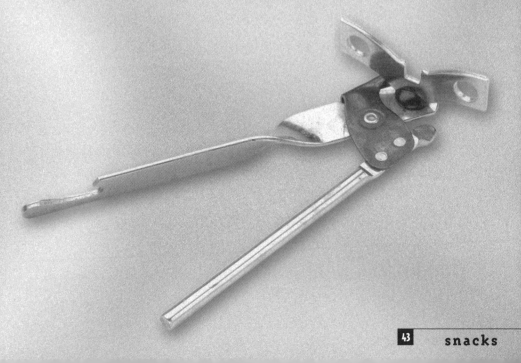

sour cream **dip**

250 g pottle sour cream
1 cup chow chow relish
2 tablespoons chopped parsley

salt and freshly ground
black pepper

∾ Mix all ingredients together in a bowl. Chill until ready to serve.

MAKES 1½ CUPS

Variations
- Use sweet fruit chutney instead of chow chow.
- Mix in ½ cup chopped fresh herbs such as mint, basil and dill, and 2 crushed garlic cloves.
- Add a packet of seafood soup and a can of shrimps to make an easy seafood dip.

guacamole (avocado dip)

1 ripe avocado
½ cup sour cream
2 teaspoons lemon juice
few drops Tabasco sauce
¼–½ teaspoon chilli powder

salt and freshly ground
black pepper
sprig of fresh herbs to garnish
(optional)

∾ Remove flesh from avocado and mash. Mix in sour cream, lemon juice, Tabasco sauce and chilli powder. Season with salt and pepper to taste. Cover. Chill until ready to serve. Garnish with a sprig of fresh herbs.

MAKES ABOUT 1 CUP

tips for busy flatters

Are you just too busy to cook every day? To make life easier and day-to-day meal preparation much less time-consuming, here are some time-saving tips for your meal preparation.

- Double a recipe up when making it. You can freeze half of the dish and save for your busier days.
- Prepare accompaniments such as mashed potato, sauces, mayonnaises, vinaigrettes, etc. ahead of time. Keep them (well labelled) in the fridge.

hummus (chickpea dip)

1 cup chickpeas	¹/₄ cup oil (preferably olive oil)
1 onion, finely chopped	2 tablespoons lemon juice
1 clove garlic, crushed	salt and freshly ground
3 tablespoons tahini	black pepper
1 teaspoon ground cumin	sprig of fresh herbs to garnish

❧ Put the chickpeas in a bowl. Cover with boiling water. Stand for 1 hour. Drain. Alternatively, cover chickpeas with plenty of cold water and soak overnight. Cook in boiling, salted water for 1 hour or until tender. Drain and allow to cool.

Put chickpeas into a food processor or blender. Add onion, garlic, tahini, cumin, oil and lemon juice. Process until smooth. Season to taste. Chill until ready to serve. Garnish with a sprig of fresh herbs. **MAKES ABOUT 1¹/₂ CUPS**

salmon and cream cheese spread

250 g cream cheese, softened	¹/₄ teaspoon cayenne pepper
200 g smoked salmon or	juice of 1 lemon
210 g can salmon, drained	freshly ground black pepper

❧ Mix all the ingredients together in a bowl or blender, until well combined. Serve spread on toasted bread or as a dip for corn chips and crostini.

MAKES 1¹/₂ CUPS

- When entertaining friends, choose recipes that can be prepared well in advance . . . that way there is more social time and less fussing in the kitchen while everyone else is enjoying themselves.
- Wash the dishes as you go. A few dishes washed and put out of the way as you cook will help ease the need for a massive clean-up at the end of meal time.
- Use your microwave to soften butter, defrost meat and steam vegetables. It will take hours off meal preparation time.

cheeseboards

 A selection of good cheeses can satisfy the tastebuds between meals. Try serving a cheeseboard as an alternative to, or as a course before, desserts — as the French do. Simplicity is the key to a well-presented cheeseboard. The following guidelines will help you to achieve a superb result.

* Offer two or three reasonable-sized pieces of cheese rather than numerous small ones that will dry out quickly and look unappetising.
* Select different types of cheese from the categories listed on page 20, for an interesting presentation.
* To ensure the cheeseboard is visually attractive, use different-shaped cheeses; for example, a wedge, a log and a cylinder of cheese.
* Remove cheese from the refrigerator at least 1 hour before serving. This allows the cheese to attain room temperature, at which the flavour is at its best.
* Keep garnishes simple — slices of crisp apple, a handful of quality shelled walnuts or a small bunch of grapes is all that is required.
* Serve unsalted crackers or sliced French or walnut bread with the cheeseboard. Place these on a separate plate. (If placed directly alongside cheese, crackers can absorb moisture and become soft.)
* For a guide to various types of cheese, see page 20.

antipasto

 Antipasto is an Italian term meaning 'before the meal' and can include any of the following types of finger food — hummus; olives; sliced meats such as salami, prosciutto, ham, smoked pork or beef; semi-dried tomatoes; feta cheese marinated in olive oil and rosemary sprigs; roasted capsicums; canned artichoke hearts; cherry tomatoes; or a small bowl of tapenade (see page 61).

Marinate olives by leaving them overnight or for a few days in flavourings of your choice. Sliced chillies, the rind of a lemon, fresh herbs or star anise can all go into the oil that olives rest in while in the jar.

Any kind of roasted vegetable can be used as can unusual breads or crackers, fresh crusty bread or crostini. Serve your antipasto platter on a nice broad plate or chopping board and garnish with edible herbs.

doorstop **toasted sandwich**

1 tablespoon olive oil
100 g mushrooms, cleaned and
  sliced
2 tablespoons parsley, finely
  chopped

3 tablespoons butter, softened
8 thick slices bread
8 slices meatloaf or ham
2 cups grated tasty cheddar cheese

Heat oil in a small frying pan. Cook mushrooms and parsley for about 3 minutes or until soft.

Butter bread. Lay 1 slice of bread butter-side down in a large frying pan. Top with meatloaf or ham, 1/4 of the mushrooms and 1/4 of the cheese. Top with another slice of bread, butter-side upwards.

Cook first side over a low heat for 6 minutes. When cheese begins to melt, use a spatula to flip the sandwich. Cook for a further 5 minutes. Repeat with the remaining slices of bread. Serve immediately.

SERVES 4

baked potatoes with sour cream and bacon

4 large potatoes
150 g sour cream
2 tablespoons butter
1 teaspoon salt

2 spring onions, sliced thinly
4 rashers bacon, chopped
  and cooked
1/2 cup grated tasty cheddar cheese

Place potatoes on an oven tray and prick with a fork. Bake at 180ºC for 40 minutes until tender.

Cut a slice from the top of each potato. Scoop out flesh, taking care not to break skin. Mash flesh until smooth. Mix in sour cream, butter, salt, spring onions and bacon. Pile into potato skins.

Replace potatoes on the oven tray and top with cheese. Heat at 200ºC for 10 minutes or until cheese is melted and golden brown.

SERVES 4

basic pizza and variations

PIZZA DOUGH
1 tablespoon Edmonds active yeast
1/2 teaspoon sugar
1 cup tepid water

1 teaspoon salt
3 cups Edmonds high grade flour
1 tablespoon oil

Combine yeast, sugar and water in a bowl. Set aside for 15 minutes or until frothy. Combine salt and flour in a large bowl. Add yeast mixture and oil. Mix to a soft dough. Transfer to a lightly floured surface and knead for 5 minutes, until smooth and elastic. Place dough in a lightly oiled large bowl and cover with a teatowel. Allow to stand in a warm place until doubled in bulk. Punch dough down in the centre, knead lightly for 1 minute and roll into a 30-cm circle. Place on a lightly greased oven tray. Top with ingredients of your choice. Cook at 220ºC for 15 minutes or until well risen and golden. **SERVES 4**

Note: To cook pizza on a pizza stone, transfer completed, uncooked pizza to a heated pizza stone and cook as above.

TOMATO SAUCE FOR PIZZA
1 tablespoon oil
1 onion, finely chopped
1 teaspoon crushed garlic
400 g can tomatoes in juice

2 tablespoons tomato paste
1 tablespoon chopped basil
salt and freshly ground black
  pepper

Heat oil in a frying pan. Cook onion for 5 minutes until soft. Add garlic, tomatoes and tomato paste, breaking up the tomatoes with a wooden spoon. Simmer for about 20 minutes until sauce is thick. Stir in basil. Season to taste.

Variations — Pizza Topping Combinations

Vegetarian Pizza
Spread the prepared pizza base with herb pesto. Top with roasted sliced eggplant, thinly sliced red onion, crumbled feta cheese, sliced cherry tomatoes and a scattering of grated mozzarella cheese.

Greek Pizza
Spread the prepared pizza base with Tomato Sauce (see above). Top with diced feta cheese, pitted halved olives, thinly sliced red onion, strips of roasted red capsicum and grated mozzarella cheese.

Chicken and Blue Cheese Pizza
Spread the prepared pizza base with herb pesto. Top with a little grated cheddar cheese, shredded cooked chicken, crumbled blue cheese, chopped walnuts and halved cherry tomatoes.

Pizza Supreme
Spread the prepared pizza base with Tomato Sauce (see above). Top with sliced salami, diced ham, anchovies, strips of roasted red capsicum, halved button mushrooms, pitted halved olives, thinly sliced red onion and grated mozzarella cheese.

Barbecue Pizza
Spread the prepared pizza base with a barbecue-style sauce. Top with sliced cooked chicken, onion rings, chopped coriander, grated cheddar or mozzarella cheese and a sprinkling of grated parmesan cheese.

Salami, Tomato and Caper Pizza
Spread the prepared pizza base with Tomato Sauce (see above). Top with sliced salami, sliced tomatoes, capers and grated mozzarella cheese.

packed pita pockets

4 pita pockets
tapenade
cheese
ham
tomato

mayonnaise
lettuce
tuna
sprouts

❧ Place whole pita bread in an oven at 180ºC for 5 minutes or microwave on High (100%) for 20 seconds. Cut the pita in half, and open to reveal the pocket. Fill with your selection of tapenade, mayonnaise, cheese, ham, tomato, lettuce, tuna, sprouts. For a simple tuna filling, mix a can of tuna with plain yoghurt and a little mint.   **SERVES 4**

Variations
*   Fill pita pockets with leftover vegetables, top with a little grated cheese and place back in the oven to melt the cheese.
*   Fill pita pockets with salads such as Couscous and Mixed Onion (page 53), Caesar (page 52), Chicken and Avocado (page 54) or hummus and guacamole (pages 45 and 44).
*   Spread a spoonful of garlic butter on the inside of each pocket and place under the grill. Toast until golden brown and crunchy, for an alternative to using French sticks as garlic bread.

sweetcorn and chilli fritters

410 g can creamed corn
pinch each of pepper and cayenne
    pepper
1 teaspoon salt
1 egg, separated

2 teaspoons sweet chilli sauce
1 tablespoon fresh chopped parsley
1 tablespoon Worcestershire sauce
1 cup Edmonds standard grade flour
oil for shallow frying

❧ Put creamed corn in a bowl and add the seasonings, egg yolk, sweet chilli sauce, parsley and Worcestershire sauce and mix. Add the flour and mix. Whisk the egg white until stiff and fold into the batter.

Heat the oil in a frying pan. Drop in spoonfuls of the mixture and brown on one side, then carefully turn over to brown the other side, about 2–3 minutes each side. Drain on kitchen paper and keep hot. Serve with extra sweet chilli sauce for dipping.   **MAKES 36**

Tip: If chilli is not for you, try using sweet fruit chutney or a pickle of your choice.

small **filo parcels**

¹/₂ cup cooked spinach, drained
150 g feta cheese, crumbled
1 egg

¹/₂ cup toasted pinenuts
8 sheets Edmonds filo pastry

꙳ Finely chop the spinach. Mix with the cheese, egg and pinenuts, using a fork to combine. To make small triangular savouries, sandwich two sheets of filo pastry together with a small amount of butter. Cut the double sheet into six strips, each about 6–7 cm wide. Put a teaspoonful of filling on the end of one strip, about a centimetre from one edge at the bottom.

Fold the corner with the filling over, so the bottom edge is against the long side, and the filling is enclosed. Keep folding the pastry over and over, until the filling is enclosed by the pastry strip. Fold any ends under, or cut them off. Brush the top surface with melted butter, and place on a lightly buttered baking sheet.

Bake the parcels at 180ºC for 10 minutes or until the pastry is crisp and golden brown. Serve immediately, or reheat when required. **MAKES 24**

Variations
* Use an alternative mixture of 150 g button mushrooms, cooked in butter with 2 tablespoons fresh, chopped parsley and 2 cloves of garlic, crushed.
* Cook 3 slices of bacon and finely dice. Mix with 150 g feta cheese and 1 large kumara, boiled and mashed. Mix together with 1 teaspoon of curry powder and season with salt and pepper.

quiche lorraine

200 g Edmonds savoury short pasty
4 eggs
1 cup milk
salt and freshly ground black pepper

4 rashers bacon, rind removed
6 spring onions

꙳ Roll pastry out on a lightly floured board and use to line a 20-cm quiche dish. Bake blind (see page 22) at 200ºC for 10 minutes. Remove baking-blind material and return pastry shell to oven for 3 minutes. Lightly beat eggs. Add milk, salt and pepper and beat to just combine. Cut bacon into strips. Trim spring onions and cut into quarters lengthwise. Sprinkle bacon over pastry base. Pour egg mixture through a sieve into pastry shell. Arrange spring onions over top of egg mixture.

Bake at 200ºC for 10 minutes, then reduce heat to 150ºC and cook for a further 20 minutes or until quiche is set. Serve hot or cold. **SERVES 4**

salads

Salads can be simple side dishes, elaborate main meals or a quick snack for your lunchbox. There are no set rules when it comes to combining ingredients for a salad. They can be simple presentations of mixed salad leaves with fresh or lightly cooked vegetables added. Or they can include cooked meats such as ham. Aim for an interesting mix of flavours and textures, such as chicken with orange, or top your salad with nuts or sunflower seeds.

A salad can provide a light meal in itself if you use pasta, potatoes or couscous as a base ingredient. Simply add vegetables, or even fruit, and finish with a tasty vinaigrette or mayonnaise.

Use your creative flair when making a dressing for your salad. Try some of the suggestions on page 56. For a simple, low-fat alternative to vinaigrette use a squeeze of lemon juice or lime juice on your salad leaves.

potato and celery salad

900 g new potatoes
2 tablespoons mint, finely chopped
2 tablespoons coriander, finely
  chopped
2 tablespoons parsley, finely
  chopped
2 cloves garlic, crushed
2 teaspoons mustard powder

juice of 1 lemon
salt and freshly ground
  black pepper
3 stalks of celery, sliced
4 eggs, hard-boiled, shelled and cut
  into quarters
mint leaves, for garnish

∽ Wash potatoes well. Cover with water and bring to the boil. Cook for about 15 minutes or until tender. Drain and allow to cool. Mix herbs, garlic, mustard powder and lemon juice in a bowl or blender to make dressing. Season to taste with salt and pepper. Arrange celery on top of potatoes on a platter. Top with eggs and dressing. Garnish with mint leaves. Chill before serving.   SERVES 4

caesar salad

4 cloves garlic, crushed
1/4 cup olive oil
3 cups cubed stale French bread
4 eggs
1 medium cos lettuce
1/4 cup lemon juice

1/2 teaspoon salt
1/4 cup olive oil
1/2 teaspoon Worcestershire sauce
1/2 cup grated or shaved parmesan
  cheese
8 anchovy fillets

∽ Mix 3 cloves of the garlic with first measure of oil so that the garlic infuses the oil. Place oil in a roasting pan. Place in a 190ºC oven for 5 minutes. Add bread cubes and toss to coat bread in oil. Bake at 190ºC for 10–15 minutes or until golden, turning occasionally.

Soft-boil eggs in boiling water (for 4 minutes). Drain and run under cold water. Wash lettuce and dry. Tear leaves into pieces and place in individual bowls or on a platter. Mix remaining garlic clove with lemon juice, salt, second measure of oil and Worcestershire sauce to make dressing.

When ready to serve, pour this dressing over lettuce. Shell eggs and chop roughly. Add to salad with bread, parmesan cheese and anchovy fillets.   SERVES 4

greek salad

1 green capsicum, deseeded and
   sliced
1 small onion, sliced
3 tomatoes, quartered
1 diced cucumber
1/2 cup pitted black olives
100 g feta cheese, cubed

DRESSING
1/4 cup olive oil
1 clove garlic, crushed
2 tablespoons spiced vinegar
1/4 teaspoon sugar

❧ Arrange capsicum, onion, tomatoes and cucumber in a salad bowl.
   To make the dressing, place all ingredients in a screw-top jar and shake
vigorously just before using. Pour dressing over the salad ingredients in the bowl
and toss to coat. Decorate with olives and feta cheese.   SERVES 4–6

couscous and mixed onion salad

2 x 355 ml cartons chicken stock
300 g couscous
2.5-cm piece root ginger, grated
4 spring onions, finely diced
2 shallots, finely diced
2 red onions, finely diced
juice and zest of 1 lime
1 tablespoon wholegrain mustard

2 cloves garlic, crushed
2 tablespoons parsley, freshly
   chopped
3/4 cup extra virgin olive oil
salt and freshly ground
   black pepper

❧ Heat stock. Place couscous in a large bowl and just cover with hot stock. Leave
to absorb stock and expand. Allow to cool. Break up with fork and fingers.
   Mix remaining ingredients into couscous. Chill until ready to serve.
                                                          SERVES 4

spinach salad

1 bunch spinach
6–8 mushrooms, sliced
2 spring onions, sliced
1 orange, peeled and segmented

3 rashers bacon, cooked and diced
$1/4$ cup Vinaigrette (see page 56)
2 hard-boiled eggs, peeled
   and chopped

෴ Tear spinach into bite-sized pieces and place in a salad bowl. Add mushrooms, spring onions, orange segments and bacon.

Chill before serving. Add Vinaigrette and toss. Garnish with eggs.

SERVES 4

chicken and avocado salad

2 avocados, peeled and sliced
2 tablespoons lemon juice
2 cups diced, chilled, cooked
   chicken or smoked chicken

$1/4$ cup cherry tomatoes
2 oranges, peeled and sliced
$1/4$ cup mayonnaise
lettuce leaves

෴ Toss avocados in lemon juice. Combine avocado, chicken, tomatoes, oranges and mayonnaise. Toss to combine. Place on a bed of lettuce leaves. Chill before serving.

SERVES 4

salad days

Wash all salad leaves thoroughly before use and leave to drain well in a colander or sieve. Store salad leaves in a sealed plastic bag in the refrigerator until ready to assemble.

coleslaw

4 cups finely shredded cabbage
1 green capsicum, deseeded and
finely sliced
1/2 cup diced celery

1 tablespoon finely chopped onion
1/4–1/2 cup Vinaigrette, Mayonnaise,
Blue Cheese dressing
(see page 56) or yoghurt

Combine cabbage, green pepper, celery and onion. Pour dressing over coleslaw. Toss to combine. Chill before serving. **SERVES 6**

Variations
Any of the following can be added:
1 cup grated carrot
1 cup grated cheese
1/2 cup chopped walnuts or peanuts
1/2 cup raisins, sultanas, chopped dates or chopped dried apricots
1 orange, peeled and diced
1/2–1 cup pineapple pieces
1 apple, finely diced
2 tablespoons chopped parsley
1 teaspoon caraway seeds

bean salad

1/2 cup dried kidney beans
1/2 cup dried haricot beans
1/2 cup dried lima beans
1/2 teaspoon salt
1/2 cup Vinaigrette (see page 56)

2 teaspoons sugar
1 clove garlic, crushed
1/4 cup chopped parsley
1 small onion, sliced

Cover beans with water and soak overnight. Drain. Cover with water and simmer gently for 40 minutes or until tender. Add salt. Drain and cool. Combine Vinaigrette, sugar and garlic. Pour this over beans. Add parsley and onion. Toss to combine. Chill for at least 2 hours before serving. **SERVES 6**

Variations
Any of the following can be added:
1 green capsicum, deseeded and finely chopped
1 cup drained whole-kernel corn
1/2 cup sliced celery

quick salad dressings

- **Mayonnaise** – Mix 1 egg yolk, $1/2$ teaspoon salt, $1/4$ teaspoon mustard, and a pinch of cayenne in a bowl. Add 1 tablespoon vinegar or lemon juice. Add oil, drop by drop, beating constantly with a whisk or beater. As mixture begins to combine, add remaining oil in a fine stream while beating. If mixture is too thick, add more vinegar. **MAKES 1 CUP**

- **Vinaigrette** – Put $3/4$ cup oil, $1/4$ cup white, wine or cider vinegar or lemon juice, $1/4$ teaspoon mustard, salt, black pepper, and 1 clove crushed garlic in a glass jar or jug. Add 1 tablespoon of chopped parsley, chives or fresh basil. Shake well to combine. **MAKES 1 CUP**

- **Blue Cheese Dressing** – Mash 50–100 g blue vein cheese with 1 cup sour cream, 1 clove crushed garlic and 2–3 tablespoons milk. Beat or blend until smooth. **MAKES 1½ CUPS**

- **Avocado Dressing** – Put $1/2$ avocado, roughly chopped, into a food processor or blender. Process until smooth. Add 1 tablespoon lime or lemon juice, $1/4$ cup oil and $1/2$ teaspoon sugar. Season to taste with salt and freshly ground black pepper. **MAKES ½ CUP**

dressing up

- Use sesame oil to give an oriental flavour to your dressing, or try walnut oil for a nutty flavour.
- Add vinegar such as balsamic vinegar instead of lemon juice or regular vinegar – this gives a richer, fuller flavour.
- Marinate vegetables such as mushrooms, tomatoes or cucumber in the dressing of your choice before adding to other ingredients.

mini meatballs with dipping sauce
top left

cheese rolls
middle

tomato soup
below

soups and starters

Making your own soups is rewarding. It is great way to use up all the spare ingredients you have left over or to make the most of vegetables when they are in season and reasonably priced.

Soup can be a meal in a bowl or a quick snack. Serve a thick soup with crusty French Garlic Bread (see page 60) and a salad and you have created a complete meal.

Traditional soups can be the basis of more adventurous dishes. Add curry or chilli powder to spice up root vegetable soups such as potato, carrot or parsnip soup.

You can add extra flavour to a creamed or canned soup by stirring in crumbled cheese before serving. Try adding a tasty cheddar cheese to onion soup or a blue cheese to a creamy mushroom soup. Or prepare small croutons as a topping for any soup (see page 62).

If you don't have a food processor to purée a soup as required in the recipe, use a ladle to push the cooked vegetables through a sieve.

Starters are designed to give your tastebuds a kick-start before the main event. They can also be used as a quick snack or light meal instead of a main meal.

tomato soup

2 teaspoons butter or oil
1 onion, finely chopped
1 stalk celery, chopped
6 medium tomatoes
salt and freshly ground
   black pepper

1/4 cup tomato paste
2 cups chicken stock
pinch of chilli powder or cayenne
   pepper
1/2 cup croutons (see page 62)

Heat butter or oil in a medium saucepan. Add onion and celery and cook until onion is clear. Blanch the tomatoes by placing them in boiling water for 30 seconds then plunging into cold water. Remove skins. Chop the flesh.

Stir the tomatoes, salt, pepper, tomato paste and stock into the onion and celery mixture. Add the chilli powder or cayenne pepper. Bring almost to the boil. Purée in blender or push through a sieve. Serve garnished with croutons.   **SERVES 4**

Tip: If you don't have fresh tomatoes use a 400 g can of tomatoes instead.

pumpkin soup

1 tablespoon oil
1 onion, chopped
750 g pumpkin, peeled and
   chopped
1 large potato, peeled and chopped

4 cups chicken stock
salt and freshly ground
   black pepper
nutmeg, to taste

Heat oil in a saucepan. Add onion and cook until clear. Add pumpkin, potato and stock. Cover, bring to the boil and cook until vegetables are soft.

Purée vegetable mixture in a blender or push through a sieve. Season with salt, pepper and nutmeg to taste. For extra flavour, a ham hock or bacon bones can be added when cooking the pumpkin.   **SERVES 4**

hot stuff

Beware of handling chillies. Always wash your hands and knife thoroughly after cutting chillies. Don't forget to remove the stalk and seeds.

mussel soup

250 g skinned and boned fish fillets	2 teaspoons chicken stock powder
4 cups water	2 tablespoons tomato paste
400 g can tomatoes in juice	1/4 teaspoon dried basil
2 tablespoons butter	16–20 fresh, cleaned mussels in
1 teaspoon curry powder	shell
2 tablespoons Edmonds standard	salt and freshly ground
grade flour	black pepper
1/4 cup dry white wine	chopped parsley to garnish

Put fish and water into a large saucepan. Bring to the boil then simmer for 15 minutes. Remove fish from pan and flake. Reserve all the liquid. Drain and chop tomatoes, reserving juice. In another saucepan, melt the butter. Add curry powder and cook for 30 seconds.

Stir in flour and cook until frothy. Gradually add reserved liquid, wine, reserved tomato juice and chicken stock powder. Bring to the boil, stirring constantly until mixture thickens slightly. Add tomato paste, basil and chopped tomatoes.

Bring back to the boil. Add mussels; simmer for 10 minutes or until mussels open. Discard any which do not open. Stir in the flaked fish, salt and pepper to taste. Serve garnished with parsley. **SERVES 4**

beef and noodle soup

1 tablespoon oil	1 red chilli, deseeded and sliced
1 onion, finely sliced	(optional)
2.5-cm piece fresh root ginger	2 1/2 cups beef stock
700 g topside steak, sliced thinly	200 g rice noodles, such as rice
100 g button mushrooms, sliced	vermicelli
2 bunches spring onions, finely	coriander leaves (or parsley), to
sliced	garnish

Heat oil in a large saucepan. Cook the onion and ginger until softened, about 5 minutes. Add the meat and cook until browned. Stir in the mushrooms, spring onions and chilli (optional). Add the beef stock and allow to come to the boil, then reduce the heat.

Place the rice noodles in a large bowl and cover with boiling water. Allow to stand. When the noodles are tender, drain, rinse and add them to the beef stock mixture. Serve immediately, garnished with coriander leaves. **SERVES 4**

french garlic bread

100 g butter, softened
2 tablespoons chopped parsley
2 cloves garlic, crushed

1/4 teaspoon salt
1 French loaf

❧ Combine butter, parsley, garlic and salt in a bowl. Cut bread diagonally into 4 pieces, then slice each piece in half lengthwise.

Preheat grill. Spread bread with garlic butter. Place under grill and toast until browned. Serve immediately.   **SERVES 4**

Tip: Any type of crusty or unsliced bread can be used. Spreading stale bread with butter and grilling to make extra crunchy toast can revive the bread.

---

cheese rolls

250 g can reduced cream
1 packet onion soup
juice of 1/2 a lemon
2 tablespoons chopped parsley

1 1/4 cups grated tasty cheddar
  cheese
12 slices sandwich-cut bread
50 g butter, melted

❧ Mix together reduced cream, onion soup, lemon juice, parsley and 1 cup of the grated cheese. Whisk well and leave to set for 10 minutes.

Cut crusts from bread. Brush one side of bread with melted butter. Spread a thin line of cheese mix on the other side. Roll up and place in an ovenproof dish. Sprinkle with remaining grated cheese.

Bake at 180ºC for 20 minutes or until cheese has melted and turned golden brown. Serve immediately.   **SERVES 4**

---

well bread

Use up any stale bread by making into toast or Garlic Bread. Loaves of stale French bread can also be used for making Crostini (see page 140). Crostini can be stored in airtight containers for 2–3 weeks.

mini **meatballs**
with dipping sauce

450 g lean minced beef
1 red onion, finely diced
2 cloves garlic, crushed
$1/2$ cup coriander leaves, finely
   chopped
1 teaspoon ground cumin
100 g pitted green olives, finely
   chopped
1 egg, beaten

salt and freshly ground
   black pepper
2 tablespoons vegetable oil

DIPPING SAUCE
4 tablespoons sweet chilli sauce
4 tablespoons tomato sauce
juice of 1 lime
1 tablespoon sesame oil
2 tablespoons soy sauce

Combine all the ingredients except the oil and shape into 40 small balls.
Place in a roasting pan with the oil and bake in a preheated oven at 190ºC for 15 minutes until well browned. To make the dipping sauce, combine all the ingredients in a glass jar. Shake well, and chill. Serve meatballs hot with the dipping sauce.

MAKES 40

tapenade

300 g black olives, pitted
3 anchovies, rinsed
3 tablespoons capers
3 tablespoons extra virgin olive oil
2 tablespoons lemon juice

2 cloves garlic, coarsely chopped
2 teaspoons fresh thyme leaves
salt and freshly ground
   black pepper

Combine all the ingredients in a food processor or blender. For a coarser spread, finely chop all ingredients together, with a sharp knife, until all are of uniform consistency. Serve with French bread or crostini (see page 140).

MAKES 1 CUP

quick soups and starters

Pea and Ham Soup
Purée a can of peas with a few pieces of bacon and ham. Heat and thin down with milk or cream. Season to taste and serve with crunchy croutons.

Chicken Noodle Soup
Add egg noodles to boiling chicken stock and a few spring vegetables and heat through. Serve with chopsticks.

Easy Minestrone
Add fresh vegetables such as mushrooms and courgettes to tomato soup and stir in some cooked macaroni elbows. Garnish with fresh herbs.

Quick Croutons
Remove crusts from bread. Cut into small squares. Heat a non-stick frying pan and toast on both sides until brown and crunchy. Alternatively, place bread pieces on an oven tray and bake at 180ºC for 5–8 minutes, turning once or twice.

Seafood Cocktail
Serve smoked mussels, surimi and shrimps in a glass with lettuce and ready-made thousand island sauce.

Goats' Cheese and Salad
Make a salad of fancy lettuce leaves and top it with pieces of goats' cheese and crispy bacon. Drizzle over Vinaigrette (see page 56).

Roasted Tomatoes
Slice tomatoes in half and bake at 150ºC for 10 minutes. Layer basil leaves and mozzarella on top and bake in the oven until cheese melts. Season with freshly ground black pepper.

quick pasta and rice

There are more than 100 different pasta shapes. Long pasta, such as spaghetti and vermicelli, and round pasta, such as macaroni and penne, are best used with olive oil and tomato-based sauces. Choose light tomato, butter or cream sauces for fine pastas and heavier, rich tomato sauces for the more robust types. Shaped pastas such as fusilli, shells and gnocchi are best used when making filling salads, or pasta pies. Broad flat pastas such as lasagne are best suited to heavy, meat-based sauces, and do not need to be cooked before baking the dish. Fettucine is an egg-based pasta and complements egg-based sauces such as carbonara.

Pasta will have their cooking times on the packet, but the general rules are simple:

1. For every 250 g of pasta use 2 litres of water and 2 teaspoons of salt.
2. Bring the water to a rolling boil and add the salt and a little oil.
3. Cook pasta until it is 'al dente' — meaning just firm to bite.
4. Rinse well in warm water before going on to the next stage of the recipe.

Rice, both long-grain and short-grain, comes in many varieties, such as arborio (short-grain and ideal for risotto), jasmine (best for spicy dishes), basmati and wild. Cooking rice perfectly just means paying attention to the grains. To avoid sticky rice, first rinse the grains under cold water until the water runs clear. Bring the water in the saucepan to a rolling boil before adding rice, and keep at a boil while the rice is cooking. Always use 3–4 times more water than the weight of the uncooked rice.

When the rice is cooked, drain and rinse it well and keep it warm over a pot of water, allowing the steam to pass through the grains. Fluff up cooked rice by separating the grains with a fork before serving.

macaroni cheese

1½ cups macaroni elbows
50 g butter
1 small onion, finely chopped
¼ cup Edmonds standard grade
    flour
½ teaspoon dry mustard

2 cups milk
2 cups grated tasty cheddar cheese
2 slices ham, diced (optional)
salt and freshly ground black
    pepper

Cook macaroni according to instructions on packet. While macaroni is cooking, make the sauce, as follows. Melt butter in a saucepan. Add onion and cook for 5 minutes until soft. Add flour and stir constantly for 2 minutes.

Remove from heat. Stir in mustard. Gradually add milk, stirring constantly. Return pan to heat, stirring continuously, until sauce thickens and comes to the boil. Remove from heat. Stir in half the cheese and the ham. Season. Add macaroni, stirring to combine.

Pour mixture into an ovenproof dish. Sprinkle over the remaining cheese. Cook at 190ºC for 20 minutes or until golden and heated through.   SERVES 4

spaghetti with chicken and peppers

2 tablespoons olive oil
3 red or yellow capsicums,
    deseeded and thinly sliced
250 g button mushrooms,
    thinly sliced
1 onion, thinly sliced

2 large cloves garlic, thinly sliced
450 g skinless, boneless chicken
    breast, thinly sliced
500 g spaghetti
1 bunch fresh basil, torn

Heat the oil in a large frying pan over a medium heat. Add the capsicums, mushrooms, onions and garlic and cook for 8–10 minutes, stirring occasionally. Add the sliced chicken breast and cook for a further 5 minutes, stirring occasionally.

Meanwhile, cook the pasta in plenty of lightly salted boiling water according to the packet instructions. Drain the pasta, reserving 25 ml of the cooking water.

Add the pasta water to the pepper mixture and stir to combine. Add the pasta to the sauce, sprinkle over basil and serve immediately.   SERVES 4

pasta marinara

1/2 cup dry white wine
1 small onion, chopped
12 fresh mussels, scrubbed and
  debearded
250 g white fish fillets e.g. gurnard,
  tarakihi, snapper
1 teaspoon oil

1 clove garlic, chopped
400 g can tomatoes in juice
100 g cooked shrimps or prawns
400 g pasta, e.g. fettucine,
  spaghetti
1/4 cup chopped parsley

Put wine, onion and mussels into a large frying pan. Cover and cook until mussels open. Remove mussels from shell. Discard any that do not open.

Add fish to pan and gently cook for 3–4 minutes or until fish flakes easily. Carefully lift fish from pan, reserving all liquid. Continue cooking the liquid until it has reduced by half.

In a separate saucepan, heat oil. Cook garlic for 30 seconds. Stir in tomatoes and their juice. Bring to the boil. Add reserved fish liquid. Mash tomatoes slightly. Reduce heat and cook uncovered until sauce thickens slightly.

Cook pasta according to instructions on packet. Drain. Stir mussels, shrimps or prawns and fish into sauce. Gently heat through. Stir in parsley. Toss sauce through hot pasta.

SERVES 4

pasta alla carbonara

2 teaspoons oil
8 rashers rindless bacon, chopped
400 g pasta shapes, e.g. penne
3 eggs
1/2 cup cream

1/2 cup freshly grated parmesan
  cheese
salt and freshly ground
  black pepper

Heat oil in a heavy-based frying pan. Cook bacon for about 6–8 minutes, stirring frequently, until almost crisp and until pan is dry. Remove from heat. Cook pasta according to instructions on packet. While pasta is cooking, whisk together eggs, cream, parmesan cheese and salt and pepper.

Drain pasta thoroughly, then return to saucepan. Toss through egg mixture and bacon. Return to a low heat and toss for 30 seconds to allow eggs to cook. Do not overheat or the egg mixture will scramble. Serve immediately. **SERVES 4**

garlic and herb **penne**

2 cups water
6 cloves garlic, peeled
100 g butter
6 tablespoons chopped parsley
3 tablespoons fresh basil,
    mint or oregano

350 g penne pasta
salt and freshly ground
    black pepper
100 g parmesan cheese

🌣 Bring the water to the boil, add the garlic and boil for 5 minutes, then drain and crush the garlic. Melt the butter and stir in the garlic, parsley and other herbs and cook over a low heat for 2 minutes.

Meanwhile, cook the penne in boiling salted water until just tender, then drain and rinse in hot water. Toss the penne in the garlic and herb butter, season to taste with salt and pepper and turn into warm serving dishes. Serve sprinkled with parmesan cheese.

SERVES 4

---

fried **rice**

1¹/₂ cups long grain rice
2 eggs
1 teaspoon soy sauce
3 tablespoons oil
6 rashers rindless bacon, chopped

1 clove garlic, crushed
2 teaspoons grated root ginger
6 spring onions, chopped
1 tablespoon soy sauce

🌣 Place rice in a sieve. Wash under cold running water to remove starch. Cook in boiling water for 12 minutes until tender. Tip into a sieve and rinse under cold running water to cool. Drain thoroughly. Spread rice out on trays and leave to dry for at least 1 hour.

Lightly beat eggs and first measure of soy sauce. Heat 1 tablespoon of the oil in a wok or heavy-based frying pan. Pour in half of the egg mixture and cook until golden on both sides. Repeat with remaining egg. Cut egg into 1-cm-wide strips. Set aside.

Heat another tablespoon of oil and cook bacon until crisp. Remove from wok. Add remaining oil to wok. Cook garlic, ginger and spring onions over a low heat for 1 minute. Add rice and stir-fry for 5 minutes. Return strips of egg and bacon to wok. Stir-fry to heat through. Add second measure of soy sauce. Stir to mix in.

SERVES 4–6

---

bacon and tomato risotto

about 6 cups chicken stock
1/4 cup olive oil
1 onion, chopped
4 rashers rindless bacon, chopped
2 cloves garlic, crushed
500 g arborio rice
1 cup dry white wine

1/2 cup freshly grated parmesan
    cheese
4 tomatoes
1/4 cup torn basil leaves
salt and freshly ground
    black pepper

❧ Bring stock to the boil in a saucepan. Heat oil in a heavy-based, deep-sided frying pan. Cook onion and bacon for 5 minutes. Add garlic and rice and stir over a low heat for 2–3 minutes to toast the rice. Add wine and cook for 1 minute.

Ladle over sufficient boiling stock to just cover the rice. Cook, stirring frequently, adding more stock to cover the rice as the liquid is absorbed. (This step will take about 18 minutes.) Remove pan from the heat. Add parmesan to the pan. Stir to combine.

Cover pan and allow to stand for 3–4 minutes. Cut tomatoes into 1-cm cubes, removing the stem end. Gently mix tomatoes and basil through the risotto. Season to taste.   SERVES 4

leek and sausage risotto

1 tablespoon oil
1 tablespoon basil
3 cloves garlic, crushed
1 packet chicken
    rice risotto

3 cups leeks, finely chopped
2–3 cooked sausages, sliced
2 1/2 cups hot water

❧ Sauté in oil, the basil, garlic and contents of the rice sachet until the rice is lightly browned. Add the leeks, sausages and hot water. Stir in the flavour sachet.

Cover and simmer over a low heat for 15 minutes. Remove lid and cook for 5 minutes or until the rice is tender. Serve immediately.   SERVES 4

Variation
For a spicier risotto, use a spicy sausage (such as chorizo) or salami. Flavoured rice risottos can be used as a quick and easy base for many meal options.

veggie cheese rice cakes

225 g arborio rice
350 g fresh spinach, washed
    and chopped
1 tablespoon water
2 tablespoons oil
1 onion, finely diced
2 tablespoons fresh, chopped
    parsley

1/4 teaspoon nutmeg
1 egg, beaten
salt and freshly ground
    black pepper
125 g blue vein cheese
175 g fresh white breadcrumbs

Cook rice in lightly salted water for 15 minutes. Place spinach in a saucepan with water. Bring to the boil and simmer for 2 minutes. Drain, refresh in cold water and squeeze out excess.

Heat 1 tablespoon of the oil in a frying pan and fry onion for 1 minute. Place in a bowl with spinach and rice. Add parsley, nutmeg and egg. Season to taste with salt and pepper. Mix well. Divide into 6 and shape into balls, placing a piece of blue vein cheese in the centre of each. Flatten balls into burger shapes. Roll in breadcrumbs. Chill for 20 minutes. Fry cakes in remaining oil in 2 batches for 3–4 minutes each side. Serve with salad.   **SERVES 2**

quick jambalaya

2 tablespoons oil
1 teaspoon paprika
225 g boneless, skinless chicken,
    cubed
150 g spicy sausage, e.g. chorizo,
    skinned and sliced
1 large onion, sliced
2 sticks celery, chopped
2 green capsicums, deseeded and
    thinly sliced

1 red capsicum, deseeded and
    thinly sliced
2 cloves garlic, crushed
300 g white long grain rice
3 1/2 cups chicken stock
2 tablespoons fresh, chopped
    parsley
2 bay leaves
2 spring onions, chopped

Heat the oil in a large frying pan. Stir in the paprika. Fry the chicken with the sausage until golden brown. Stir in the onion, celery, capsicum and garlic. Fry until the vegetables begin to soften. Add the rice and stir for 2 minutes.

Pour over the stock and add the parsley and bay leaves. Bring to the boil and cover tightly, simmering for 10 minutes. Turn off the heat and leave for about 20 minutes until all the liquid has been absorbed. Serve garnished with chopped spring onions and a tossed green salad.   **SERVES 4–6**

main meals
with meat

Meat can prove prohibitively expensive on a tight budget. But buying cheaper cuts of meat can sometimes be a false economy. Cheaper cuts often include a lot of bone and fat. There is very little waste on quality cuts of meat, and they may prove to be better value, as well as being more delicious. Always ask your butcher to cut away any excess fat or skin.

Checking for done-ness

As a rule, red meats such as lamb, beef, or venison are at their best when the meat is slightly pink when cooked. It is a matter of personal taste as to how much or how little you cook your piece of meat. (See guidelines for cooking times on page 31.) Chicken should not be pink when eaten. The meat should be white. Pork can be eaten slightly pink, but any juices must run clear.

To test meat, insert a skewer or knife into the thickest or densest part of the meat. In a chicken this is around the breast and through to the rib cage. For steak, this is in the middle, and for a rolled roast this will be the thickest middle section. If the juices run clear and don't have any sign of pinkness, that will generally mean the meat is cooked through.

With a steak you may not want the juices to run clear. To help you perfect the art of telling whether a steak is cooked exactly the way you like it, time the cooking period and set a standard in that way. It is better to undercook than to overcook meat; if you undercook it and it is still not of the desired tenderness then it can be re-cooked.

quick **burgers**

BURGER PATTIES	1 egg, lightly beaten
750 g lean beef mince	salt and freshly ground
250 g sausage meat	black pepper
1 onion, finely chopped	2 tablespoons oil
1 tablespoon Worcestershire sauce	
2 tablespoons tomato sauce	8 burger buns
1 cup fresh white breadcrumbs	toppings

 Place beef mince and sausage meat in a large bowl. Add onion, sauces, breadcrumbs, egg and seasonings. Using hands, mix until thoroughly combined. Divide mixture into 8 equal portions and shape into 1.5-cm thick patties. Refrigerate patties for at least 30 minutes.

Heat oil in a large frying pan. Place patties in the pan and fry on each side for 8 minutes. To assemble burgers, split the burger buns and toast under the grill. Top each bun with a cooked burger pattie and then the topping of your choice.

SERVES 4

Toppings

- **Kiwi-style** — Assemble with slices of beetroot, tomato, onions, cheese, lettuce and tomato sauce or relish.
- **Asian** — Stir fry spring vegetables with some shredded cabbage leaves. Flavour with soy sauce and hoisin sauce.
- **American** — Melt slices of cheese onto the burger buns, spread with tomato sauce and mustard and top with gherkins and fried onions.
- **Middle Eastern** — Make couscous salad (page 53) and use to top the burger bun or use pita bread. Top with yoghurt and ready-made barbecue sauce.

Burger-meister

Burgers can be prepared up to 4 hours in advance and stored, covered, in the fridge, or placed between pieces of greaseproof paper and put in a plastic bag or container. Freeze for up to 3–4 months. Remember to label and date the bag for easy identification.

beef and bean burritos

MEAT MIXTURE
1 tablespoon oil
2 onions, chopped
1 clove garlic, crushed
1 red capsicum, deseeded
   and chopped
500 g lean beef mince
1½ teaspoons chilli powder
1 cup water
300 g can tomato purée

salt and freshly ground
   black pepper
465 g can red kidney beans

8 flour tortillas
Guacamole (see page 44)
1 cup grated tasty cheddar cheese
2 tomatoes, sliced
lettuce and sour cream to serve

Heat oil in a large frying pan or saucepan. Add onions, garlic and red capsicum. Cook until onion is clear. Stir in meat and cook until meat is browned. Add chilli powder, water, tomato purée, and season with salt and pepper to taste. Bring to the boil, stirring constantly. Reduce heat and simmer gently for 30 minutes or until mixture is quite thick. Drain beans. Add to pan. Continue cooking for a further 10 minutes, stirring occasionally.

Warm tortillas in the oven. Lay each tortilla flat and top with a spoonful of meat mixture, then a spoonful of Guacamole, cheese and slices of tomato. Fold the edges of the tortilla into the centre to make a parcel. Place burritos on a baking tray and heat through in moderate oven. Serve with shredded lettuce and sour cream. **SERVES 4**

chilli con carne

1 tablespoon oil
2 onions, chopped
1 clove garlic, crushed
1 green capsicum, deseeded
   and chopped
500 g lean beef mince
1½ teaspoons chilli powder

50 g dark chocolate
1 cup water
300 g can tomato purée
¼ teaspoon oregano
salt and freshly ground
   black pepper
465 g can red kidney beans

Heat oil in a large frying pan or saucepan. Add onions, garlic and green capsicum. Cook until onion is clear. Stir in meat and cook until meat is browned. Add chilli powder, dark chocolate, water, tomato purée and oregano, and season with salt and pepper to taste. Bring to the boil, stirring constantly.

Reduce heat and simmer gently for 30 minutes or until mixture is quite thick. Drain beans. Add to pan. Continue cooking for a further 10 minutes, stirring occasionally. **SERVES 4**

bolognese sauce with spaghetti

1 tablespoon oil	1 teaspoon dried oregano
1 large onion, finely chopped	1¹/₂ cups water
500 g lean beef mince	salt and freshly ground
¹/₄ cup tomato paste	black pepper
400 g can tomatoes in juice	400 g spaghetti
1 teaspoon dried basil	grated parmesan cheese to serve

To make sauce, heat oil in a large frying pan. Add onion and cook for 5 minutes until soft. Stir in meat and quickly brown. Add tomato paste and tomatoes in juice, breaking up the tomatoes with a wooden spoon. Stir in herbs and water.

Bring to the boil, reduce heat and simmer for 25–30 minutes or until mixture is of a thick sauce consistency. Season to taste. Cook spaghetti according to instructions on packet. Drain. Arrange on serving plate and top with Bolognese Sauce. Garnish with parmesan cheese. **SERVES 4**

lasagne with spinach and feta

2 tablespoons oil	¹/₂ teaspoon dried basil
1 onion, chopped	1 teaspoon sugar
3 cloves garlic, crushed	salt and freshly ground
500 g lean beef mince	black pepper
100 g mushrooms, sliced	400 g frozen spinach
2 x 400 g cans tomatoes in juice,	250 g feta cheese
chopped	250 g lasagne, cooked
1 cup tomato purée	¹/₂ cup tomato sauce
1 teaspoon dried oregano	³/₄ cup grated tasty cheddar cheese

Heat oil in a large frying pan. Add onion and garlic. Cook until onion is golden. Increase heat. Add meat and brown well. Add mushrooms, tomatoes in juice, tomato purée, oregano, basil and sugar. Stir. Bring to the boil then reduce heat and simmer gently for 40 minutes or until meat mixture has thickened slightly, stirring occasionally. Season with salt and pepper to taste. Set aside until cool. Squeeze the moisture out of the defrosted spinach. Cut the feta cheese into thin slices. Place ¹/₃ of the lasagne in a greased ovenproof dish. Spread with half the meat mixture and then top with the spinach. Place another layer of lasagne over the spinach. Top with the remaining meat mixture then lay the feta cheese slices on top of that. Place the final pieces of lasagne on top. Spread over the tomato sauce. Top with the grated cheese. Cook at 180ºC for 20 minutes or until golden and heated through.

SERVES 4–6

beef and vegetable stir-fry

3 tablespoons olive oil
350 g steak, cut into strips
6 spring onions, sliced
1 clove garlic, chopped
1 red capsicum, deseeded and cut
   into strips
1 yellow capsicum, deseeded and
   cut into strips
175 g carrots, cut into strips

425 g can baby corn, drained
1 teaspoon Edmonds Fielder's
   cornflour
5 tablespoons fish sauce
2 tablespoons soy sauce
3/4 cup beef stock
100 g bean sprouts
salt and freshly ground
   black pepper

Heat oil in a large wok or frying pan and fry steak for 3 minutes or until browned. Remove from frying pan and keep warm. Fry spring onions, garlic, red and yellow capsicums, carrots and baby corn for 3 minutes.

Mix cornflour with fish sauce and soy sauce. Add to frying pan and bring to the boil; keep stirring until sauce thickens. Stir in stock, bean sprouts and steak. Season to taste with salt and pepper. Heat through. Serve with steamed white rice.

SERVES 4

shepherd's pie with kumara topping

1 tablespoon oil
1 onion, chopped
500 g lean beef mince
2 tablespoons Edmonds standard
   grade flour
1 tablespoon tomato sauce
1 tablespoon sweet fruit chutney

3/4 cup liquid beef stock
4 kumara, peeled and chopped
1 tablespoon butter
1 small onion, finely chopped
1/2 cup grated tasty cheddar cheese
salt and freshly ground
   black pepper

Heat oil in a large frying pan. Add first onion and cook until clear. Add mince and cook until well browned, stirring constantly. Stir in flour and cook for 1 minute. Add tomato sauce, chutney and stock. Bring to the boil, reduce heat and simmer for 5 minutes. Set aside. Cook kumara in boiling, salted water until tender. Drain and heat for a few minutes to dry off excess moisture. Shake pan frequently during this time. Mash kumara. Add butter, second onion and half of the cheese, mixing until smooth and creamy. Season with salt and pepper to taste.

Put mince into a pie dish. Top with kumara mixture. Sprinkle with remaining cheese. Bake at 190ºC for 20 minutes or until golden and heated through.

SERVES 4

oriental beef and ginger casserole

1 tablespoon olive oil
1 clove garlic, crushed
1 onion, sliced
600 g diced braising steak
100 g button mushrooms
2 carrots, sliced

2 tablespoons of grated root ginger
1 tablespoon soy sauce
1 tablespoon clear honey
355 ml carton beef stock
salt and freshly ground
   black pepper

Heat oil in a large frying pan. Cook garlic and onion for 2 minutes or until softened. Add beef and brown for 5 minutes.

Preheat oven to 160ºC. Place onions, garlic and beef in a large casserole dish with mushrooms, carrots, ginger, soy sauce, honey and stock. Season well with salt and pepper. Cover and cook for 1½–2 hours.   **SERVES 4**

bœuf bourguignon

750 g chuck steak
2 tablespoons Edmonds standard
   grade flour
salt and freshly ground
   black pepper
2 tablespoons oil
8 pickling onions
2 rashers bacon

2 cloves garlic, crushed
¾ cup red wine
½ cup beef stock
4 carrots, quartered lengthwise
sprig parsley
sprig thyme
bay leaf

Trim fat from meat. Cut meat into serving-sized pieces. Combine flour, salt and pepper. Coat meat in seasoned flour. Heat oil in a flameproof casserole dish. Add onions and bacon and cook until golden. Using a slotted spoon, remove from pan and set aside.

Add half the meat to pan and quickly brown on all sides. Repeat with remaining meat. Return onions and bacon to pan with garlic. Add wine and stock, stirring well. Add carrots. Make a bouquet garni from parsley, thyme and bay leaf (see page 22). Add to casserole.

Cover and cook at 180ºC for 1½–2 hours or until meat is tender. Serve with French bread and salad.   **SERVES 4**

lamb satay

4 lean lamb leg steaks
1 tablespoon chopped coriander
2 teaspoons oil
1 teaspoon sambal oelek or chilli
  paste
bamboo skewers soaked in cold
  water for 30 minutes

SAUCE
1/4 cup soy sauce
1/4 cup chopped spring onions
1 teaspoon sambal oelek or chilli
  paste
2 tablespoons lemon or lime juice

๑ Trim fat from meat, cut meat into small cubes and put in a bowl. Add coriander, oil and first measure of sambal oelek. Leave to marinate for 30 minutes. Thread meat onto soaked bamboo skewers.

Grill for 10 minutes or until just cooked, turning occasionally. Serve with sauce. To make the sauce, combine all ingredients.   **SERVES 4**

rack of lamb with honey

1 rack of lamb (about 350 g),
  trimmed
salt and freshly ground
  black pepper
1 teaspoon oil
50 g butter, chilled
1 small onion, finely chopped

1/3 cup vegetable stock
juice of 1/2 an orange
1 teaspoon grated root ginger
25 g cashew nuts
25 g raisins
2 tablespoons honey

๑ Preheat oven to 240ºC. Season lamb with salt and pepper. Place in a roasting pan and cook for 15–20 minutes for medium-cooked lamb or 25–30 minutes for well-done lamb.

While lamb cooks, to make sauce, heat oil and half the butter in a large frying pan. Add onion and cook for 3 minutes, stirring constantly. Add stock, orange juice, ginger, cashew nuts, raisins and honey. Bring to the boil and simmer for 5 minutes.

Cut remaining chilled butter into small pieces. Add to sauce a little at a time, whisking well after each addition and keeping sauce at a gentle simmer. Remove lamb from oven and leave to rest in a warm place for 5 minutes.

Carve rested lamb into cutlets. Serve immediately with sauce and steamed baby vegetables.   **SERVES 2**

snappy lamb hot pot

2 tablespoons olive oil
1 onion, sliced
2 garlic cloves, sliced
500 g lamb leg steaks, diced
400 g can tomatoes in juice

250 g green beans, trimmed and
  halved
1 teaspoon mixed dried herbs
500 g potatoes, very thinly sliced
1 teaspoon salt
freshly ground black pepper

Heat oil in a 25-cm-diameter frying pan with a lid. Add onion and garlic and cook, stirring, until golden. Push to one side and add lamb. Cook, turning once, for 5–6 minutes until browned.

Add tomatoes, beans and herbs. Bring to the boil, stirring, then reduce heat.

Arrange potato slices in overlapping layers on top of lamb. Season to taste with salt and pepper. Simmer, covered, for 20 minutes until lamb and potatoes are tender. Preheat grill to high. Place hot pot under grill and brown before serving.

SERVES 4

moroccan lamb stew

2 tablespoons vegetable oil
1 onion, sliced
2 garlic cloves, crushed
700 g boneless lamb, diced
2 tablespoons Edmonds standard
  grade flour
salt and freshly ground
  black pepper

2³/4 cups vegetable stock
1 tablespoon tomato purée
1 lemon
2 tablespoons pitted black olives
1 red capsicum, deseeded
  and chopped
1/4 cup roughly chopped parsley
couscous, to serve

Heat the oil in a large pan, and then fry the onion and garlic for 4-5 minutes until just golden. Combine flour, salt and pepper in a bowl. Coat meat in seasoned flour. Fry, turning frequently, until starting to brown.

Stir in the stock and tomato purée. Bring just to the boil, then reduce the heat, cover and simmer gently for 1 hour until the meat is just tender and the sauce is slightly thickened. Slice off two strips of rind from the lemon and squeeze its juice. Stir the rind strips and juice into the stew with the olives and the red capsicum.

Cook over a gentle heat for 7–8 minutes until the capsicum is just cooked. Season with salt and pepper if necessary, then stir in the parsley. Cool, transfer to a non-metallic container and cover; chill overnight. Tip the stew into a large pan and reheat gently for 20 minutes. Serve on a bed of couscous.   SERVES 4

lamb curry

1¹/2 tablespoons Edmonds standard
   grade flour
salt and freshly ground
   black pepper
750 g lamb pieces
oil
1 large onion, chopped
2 cloves garlic, crushed

1 tablespoon tomato paste
1¹/2 teaspoons grated root ginger
1 teaspoon chopped fresh chilli
1¹/2 teaspoons ground cumin
1 teaspoon ground coriander
1 teaspoon ground cardamom
¹/2 cup chicken stock

Combine flour, salt and pepper in a bowl. Coat meat in seasoned flour. Set aside. Heat oil in a large saucepan.

Add onion and garlic to pan and cook until onion is clear. Remove with slotted spoon. Add half of the meat to pan and quickly brown all over. Remove from pan and repeat with remaining meat.

Return meat and onion mixture to saucepan. Add tomato paste, ginger, chilli, cumin, coriander, cardamom and stock, stirring well. Bring to the boil.

Cover, reduce heat and simmer gently for 1 hour or until meat is tender. Serve with cucumber salad and poppadoms.

SERVES 4

stuffed lamb cutlets

8 lamb cutlets
2 slices pressed ham
¹/4 cup grated tasty cheddar cheese
¹/4 cup Edmonds standard grade
   flour
¹/2 teaspoon salt

freshly ground black pepper
1 egg
2 tablespoons water
³/4 cup dry breadcrumbs
oil for frying

Cut each cutlet horizontally almost through to bone. Open out to resemble butterfly wings. Cut ham into eighths. Place a piece of ham on cut side of meat. Top with a small amount of cheese. Close cutlet again to completely encase filling.

Combine flour, salt and pepper to taste. Dip lamb into the seasoned flour. Beat egg and water together. Dip lamb in egg mixture, then in breadcrumbs, shaking off the excess. Repeat egg-and-breadcrumbs step for each cutlet. Heat oil in a frying pan.

Fry lamb for 5 minutes on each side or until golden. Drain on absorbent paper. Serve hot with mashed potato.

SERVES 4

roast leg of lamb
with orange and mint

1.5–2 kg whole leg of lamb
1 orange
2–3 garlic cloves, peeled
2–3 mint sprigs

salt and freshly ground
black pepper
3 tablespoons olive oil
150 g apricot jam

Trim off any excess fat from the lamb – do keep some of the fat on because it makes the meat more tender. Make 10–12 incisions into the top side of the meat with a sharp knife.

Cut the rind off the orange and slice into thin strips; try not to get too much of the white pith. Cut the garlic cloves into thin strips. Push the orange rind, garlic pieces and a couple of mint leaves into each slit. Season the olive oil and pour it over the lamb. Place the meat in a roasting pan and cover with another roasting pan as a lid, or with foil.

Roast at 180ºC for 55 minutes per 1 kg, plus 25 minutes. In the last 35 minutes, remove the foil or lid and allow the meat to brown. Heat the apricot jam in a small saucepan. Pour over the meat joint as it comes out of the oven. Allow the joint to rest in a warm place before carving. **SERVES 8**

Variations

- Use different jams, such as blackberry, boysenberry or marmalade.
- Use different herbs, such as rosemary or sage, instead of mint.
- Instead of inserting herbs and citrus, make the incisions and press small spoonfuls of pesto (basil or mint) into the lamb.

marinated **chicken wings**

3 cloves garlic, crushed
3 tablespoons soy sauce
2 tablespoons liquid honey

1 tablespoon tomato sauce
2 teaspoons grated root ginger
12 chicken wings

Combine garlic, soy sauce, honey, tomato sauce and ginger. Brush the chicken wings with this mixture. Leave to marinate for 1 hour.

Grill for 8–10 minutes or until golden, turning once during cooking time. Alternatively, place wings in roasting pan and cook at 200ºC for about 15 minutes or until crisp and golden. Serve hot or cold. **SERVES 4**

cheese and sesame-coated **chicken**

8 chicken drumsticks
2 tablespoons Edmonds standard
  grade flour
2 tablespoons grated parmesan
  cheese

1 teaspoon chicken stock powder
$1/4$ teaspoon mixed herbs
2 tablespoons dry breadcrumbs
2 teaspoons sesame seeds
oil

Remove skin from chicken. Moisten chicken slightly with water. Combine flour, parmesan cheese, stock powder, herbs, breadcrumbs and sesame seeds. Put this mixture into a plastic bag. Add 2 drumsticks to bag and shake to coat. Repeat with remaining chicken, coating only 2 at a time.

Place drumsticks in a lightly oiled baking dish. Allow to stand for 15 minutes. Cook at 200ºC for 25 minutes, or until juices run clear when tested. Turn chicken once or twice during the cooking time. Serve hot or cold. **SERVES 4**

apricot and coconut
chicken drumsticks

100 g apricot jam	8 chicken drumsticks
1/4 cup orange juice	100 g desiccated coconut

Preheat oven to 190ºC. Warm apricot jam and mix with orange juice. Brush liberally over drumsticks. Coat in coconut.

Place in a roasting pan. Cook for 30 minutes, turning once or twice, until golden and cooked through.   **SERVES 4**

simple chicken stroganoff

1 tablespoon oil	3 teaspoons Dijon mustard
1 large onion, sliced	salt and freshly ground
800 g skinned and boned chicken	black pepper
thighs	2 spring onions, finely sliced
3/4 cup dry white wine	
250 g button mushrooms	
(about 12)	
250 g crème fraîche	

Heat oil in a large frying pan. Add onion and cook for 2 minutes until onion has softened. Cut each chicken thigh into 6 pieces. Add chicken to frying pan. Cook for a further 5 minutes or until chicken is golden. Pour in wine and cook until liquid is reduced by half.

Add mushrooms, crème fraîche and mustard to frying pan. Add salt and pepper. Cook for a further 5 minutes or until chicken is cooked through and sauce has thickened. Add spring onions. Serve with potato wedges (see page 109) and sautéed courgettes (see page 112).

                                        SERVES 4

chicken **enchiladas**

400 g can tomatoes in juice
113 g can jalapeño peppers
1 teaspoon ground coriander
1/2 teaspoon salt
250 g sour cream
2 tablespoons oil
2 cups chopped, cooked chicken

1 small onion, finely chopped
salt and freshly ground
    black pepper
8 x 20-cm-diameter flour tortillas
3/4 cup grated tasty cheddar cheese

Put tomatoes with their juice, jalapeño peppers, coriander and salt into a food processor or blender. Process until smooth. Add sour cream and process to combine. Set aside. Heat oil in a saucepan. Add chicken and onion. Cook for about 5 minutes, stirring constantly, until onion is soft. Season to taste with salt and pepper.

Lay tortillas on a flat surface. Spread with tomato mixture. Divide chicken mixture between the tortillas, spreading in a log shape along one edge. Roll up like a sponge roll. Place seam side down in ovenproof dish. Repeat with remaining tortillas and chicken.

Pour remaining tomato mixture over. Sprinkle with cheese. Cover dish with lid or foil. Cook at 180ºC for 30 minutes. Remove lid, then grill until golden.

SERVES 4

thai **chicken salad**

1/4 cup oil
1 small onion, thinly sliced
2 cloves garlic, thinly sliced
450 g cooked chicken, skinned and
    thinly sliced
1 carrot, cut into matchsticks
8 cherry tomatoes, quartered
5 spring onions, finely sliced
1 red onion, thinly sliced

1 bunch freshly chopped mint
1 bunch freshly chopped coriander

SAUCE
2 limes, juice only
3 tablespoons fish sauce
2 tablespoons red chilli flakes
50 g peanuts, chopped, to garnish

Heat the oil in a large frying pan until very hot. Add the onion and garlic and cook for 4–5 minutes or until golden and crispy. Remove from pan and drain on kitchen paper. Set aside. In a bowl, toss together the chicken, carrot, tomatoes, spring onions, red onion, mint and coriander. Set aside.

In a small bowl, mix together all the sauce ingredients. Pour over the salad and toss. Arrange the salad on serving plates. To garnish, sprinkle with the peanuts and reserved onions and garlic.

SERVES 4

chicken chop suey

350 g egg noodles
2 tablespoons oil
4 small skinless, boneless chicken
    breasts, thinly sliced diagonally
salt and freshly ground
    black pepper
1 bunch spring onions, trimmed
    and halved lengthways

1 clove garlic, sliced
150 g button mushrooms, sliced
5 tablespoons oyster sauce
$^1/_2$ cup chicken stock
200 g cabbage leaves or Chinese
    cabbage leaves

Cook egg noodles in boiling water for 6 minutes. Drain and keep warm.

Heat oil in a frying pan. Add chicken. Season to taste with salt and pepper. Cook on high heat for 3–4 minutes until browned and almost cooked through. Add spring onions, garlic, mushrooms and more pepper, if desired. Cook, stirring, for 2 minutes.

Add oyster sauce and stock, stirring to heat through. Add cabbage and cook for 1–2 minutes until just wilted. Check seasoning and add salt, if desired. Serve on a bed of warm egg noodles. **SERVES 4**

chicken paprika

4 chicken breasts
2 tablespoons oil
1 large onion, chopped
2 teaspoons paprika
1 tablespoon Edmonds standard
    grade flour

1 cup chicken stock
250 g pot sour cream or
    1 cup cream
1 tablespoon lemon juice
salt and freshly ground
    black pepper

Remove skin and fat from chicken. Heat oil in a large frying pan. Add chicken and quickly brown on all sides. Remove from pan and set aside. Add onion to pan and cook until clear. Stir in paprika and cook for 30 seconds.

Stir in flour and cook, stirring, for 1 minute. Gradually add stock, stirring constantly. Bring to the boil. Return chicken to pan. Cover, reduce heat and simmer gently for 15 minutes. Stir in sour cream.

Continue cooking gently for a further 10 minutes or until juices run clear when tested. Add lemon juice. Season with salt and pepper to taste. Serve with rice. **SERVES 4**

roast chicken
with lemon and rice stuffing

250 g rice
1 tablespoon olive oil
1 onion, finely sliced
2 cloves garlic, finely diced
4 large sage leaves, chopped

juice and zest of 1 lemon
1 x No.18 chicken
2 tablespoons butter, melted
4–5 lemon slices

✿ Stuffing
Cook rice in boiling, salted water for 12 minutes until softened. Drain well. Heat oil in a frying pan. Add onion and cook until softened. Add garlic, sage and lemon zest and cook for 2 minutes. Mix in rice, stirring well. Allow stuffing to cool.

Preparation
Remove giblets from chicken. Rinse out cavity with cold running water. Drain. Pat chicken dry with paper towels. Spoon stuffing into cavity. Close the cavity using a wooden skewer. Cross legs of chicken and tie with string, including the parson's nose, so the legs are neatly placed over the chicken.

Mix lemon juice and butter. Rub over top of chicken. Arrange lemon slices on top and hold in place with toothpicks.

Roast, basting occasionally and covering loosely with foil when chicken turns golden. Cook in 190ºC oven for 2½ hours or until juices run clear when thigh is pierced with a knife. Leave to stand for 15 minutes before carving.

SERVES 4–6

Variations
- **Wild rice and cashew nut stuffing**: ½ cup cooked wild rice; 1 tablespoon oil; 1 onion finely chopped; 1 teaspoon crushed garlic; 100 g button mushrooms, sliced; ½ cup fresh breadcrumbs; ½ cup roughly chopped cashew nuts; 1 egg; salt and freshly ground black pepper to season. Cook onion for 5 minutes until softened. Add garlic and mushrooms and cook for 6–8 minutes. Combine all remaining ingredients in a bowl. Mix well. Spoon stuffing into chicken cavity, and cook as above.

- **Cheat's stuffing**: 2 onions, peeled and cut into quarters; 1 lemon cut into quarters – stuff onion and lemon pieces into the cavity of the chicken. Roast as above.

hot and spicy **pork ribs**

6 tablespoons tomato sauce
1/4 cup Worcestershire sauce
2 tablespoons Dijon mustard
a splash of Tabasco sauce or pinch
  of chilli powder

4 tablespoons brown sugar
12–16 pork spare ribs

Heat a barbecue or preheat grill. Mix together tomato sauce, Worcestershire sauce, mustard, Tabasco sauce or chilli powder, and sugar. Brush over pork.

Grill or barbecue for 20 minutes, basting with some of the sauce every 5 minutes and turning once.

Remove pork ribs and heat the remaining sauce for 3 minutes, until heated through. Drizzle over pork. Serve with garlic bread and a salad.   **SERVES 2**

creamy **lemon pork**

750 g diced pork fillet
20 g butter
250 g button mushrooms, sliced
1 cup chicken stock
250 g pot crème fraîche
1 tablespoon lemon juice

salt and freshly ground
  black pepper
1/2 a small lemon, cut into small
  wedges
parsley, to garnish

Trim pork of excess fat and sinew. Heat butter in heavy-based frying pan. Cook pork in small batches over a medium-high heat until well browned. Drain on absorbent paper.

Add mushrooms to frying pan and cook for 2 minutes. Return pork to frying pan. Add stock and bring to the boil. Reduce heat and simmer, covered, for 30 minutes or until meat is tender, stirring occasionally.

Add crème fraîche to frying pan, increase heat and stir until sauce thickens. Simmer for 2 minutes. Season with lemon juice, salt and pepper. Decorate with lemon wedges and parsley and serve with noodles.   **SERVES 4**

sweet and sour **pork**

500 g pork pieces
2 cloves garlic, crushed
2 tablespoons oil
2 small onions, quartered
1/2 cup chicken stock
225 g can pineapple pieces in syrup
1 tablespoon Edmonds Fielder's
   cornflour
1/4 cup tomato sauce

1/2 teaspoon grated root ginger
2 tablespoons white vinegar
2 tablespoons brown sugar
1/2 red capsicum, deseeded and
   chopped
1/2 cup chopped cucumber
1/2 cup baby sweetcorn
100 g mushrooms, quartered

Trim fat from pork and cut meat into 2-cm pieces. Peel garlic and chop finely. Heat oil in a saucepan or wok. Add onion and garlic and cook until onion is clear. Remove from pan. Add half the pork pieces to pan and quickly brown on all sides, then remove from pan. Repeat with remaining meat.

Return meat and onion mixture to pan. Add stock and bring to the boil. Cover and cook gently for 30 minutes or until meat is tender. Drain pineapple, reserving juice.

Combine pineapple juice and cornflour, mixing until smooth. Add pineapple pieces, tomato sauce, ginger, vinegar, sugar, capsicum, cucumber, sweetcorn and mushrooms to pan. Cook for 5 minutes. Return to the boil. Stir in cornflour mixture and boil for 2 minutes or until mixture thickens slightly. Serve with rice or noodles.

SERVES 4

baked pork chops
with honey and mustard

4 large bone-in pork chops
a little oil, for brushing
2 cloves garlic, peeled and crushed
2 tablespoons Worcestershire sauce
2 tablespoons tomato purée

1 teaspoon chilli sauce
2 tablespoons lemon juice
3 tablespoons wholegrain mustard
1/4 cup liquid honey

Rub or brush chops with oil. Heat a non-stick frying pan and fry chops on both sides until golden. Transfer to a shallow baking dish.

Mix remaining ingredients. Stir mixture. Pour over chops. Cook at 200ºC for 40 minutes, basting (see page 22) occasionally until sauce is thick and shiny. Serve chops coated with sauce, accompanied with mashed potatoes and green beans.

SERVES 4

roast loin of pork
with garlic crackling

1.5 kg boneless loin of pork
2 tablespoons oil
2 tablespoons sea salt
1 teaspoon black pepper
4 garlic cloves, halved

few sprigs fresh rosemary
4 granny smith apples, halved
4 flat mushrooms, sliced
25 g butter

Score the pork skin vertically in thin strips with a very sharp knife. Rub the skin with oil, salt and pepper. Insert pieces of garlic into the pork flesh. Roll up and tie with string.

Put meat on top of the sprigs of rosemary in a roasting pan and cook in 220ºC oven for 25 minutes until skin bubbles and crackling has formed. Reduce the oven temperature to 190ºC. Cook for another 1 hour 15 minutes. To roast pork, calculate 25 minutes per 450 g plus the 25 minutes at the start. Add the apples and mushrooms to the roasting pan 30 minutes before end of cooking period.

Remove pork, apples and mushrooms from the roasting pan. Place pan on element and bubble up the juices, skimming off any excess fat and scraping up the sediment. Add butter and 1/2 cup boiling water. Bring to the boil for a few minutes and season. Return the mushrooms to the dish to heat through.

Remove crackling to be carved separately, carve the pork and serve with the apples, and fresh, steamed vegetables. **SERVES 4-6**

know your onions

To soften or sauté an onion, bring the oil to a high temperature. Add the onions and then turn down the heat and allow to cook or 'sweat' out the natural juices. Slowly cooking onions will bring out the sweetness. Try not to burn or blacken them because this will cause bitterness in your final dish.

meatloaf

500 g lean beef mince
500 g sausage meat
1 onion, finely chopped
2 cloves garlic, crushed
1 egg
1 cup grated carrot
1/2 cup chopped parsley
2 teaspoons prepared mustard
2 teaspoons mixed herbs

1 teaspoon salt
black pepper

TOPPING
1/4 cup rolled oats
2 tablespoons brown sugar
1/4 cup tomato sauce
1/4 cup chopped parsley

Combine mince, sausage meat, onion, garlic, egg, carrot, parsley, mustard and herbs, with salt and pepper to taste. Mix well. Press mixture into a 22-cm loaf tin. Combine all topping ingredients and spread evenly over top of meatloaf.

Cover with foil and cook at 190ºC for 30 minutes. Remove foil and cook for a further 30 minutes or until juices run clear when tested with a skewer. Serve hot or cold. **SERVES 4–6**

marsala curry sausages

12 sausages
2 tablespoons oil
4 onions, thinly sliced
2 cloves garlic, finely chopped
3 tablespoons grated root ginger
1 tablespoon turmeric

1 teaspoon cayenne pepper
1 teaspoon ground cumin
400 g can tomatoes in juice, chopped
355 ml carton beef stock
1 teaspoon salt
coriander or Italian parsley, to garnish

Cook sausages in a roasting pan or grill tray for 10–12 minutes at 200ºC. Heat oil in a large frying pan or saucepan. Add onions and cook for 5 minutes until softened. Add garlic, ginger, turmeric, cayenne pepper and cumin and cook for another 10 minutes on a low heat until onions turn golden brown.

Add tomatoes, stock and salt and bring to the boil. Reduce heat and simmer for 20 minutes. When sauce has reduced, turn heat to low. Slice sausages into 1-cm pieces. Add to tomato sauce and cook for 15 minutes. Serve garnished with fresh coriander or Italian parsley on steamed white rice. **SERVES 4**

sausages in red wine gravy

2 onions
2 tablespoons vegetable oil
8 sausages
1 cup red wine

3 tablespoons port wine jelly
salt and freshly ground
   black pepper

Thinly slice onions. Heat oil in a large frying pan. Add onions and fry for about 5 minutes until they start to brown around the edges.

Using a slotted spoon, transfer onions to a plate. Add sausages to the frying pan. Cook, turning regularly for about 10 minutes until they are brown all over.

Return onions and their juices to the frying pan. Stir in wine and jelly. Season to taste with salt and pepper. Bring to the boil, then reduce heat and simmer sauce for 10 minutes until it thickens. If sauce fails to thicken, remove sausages and keep warm. Boil sauce until it thickens. Pour over sausages and serve with mashed potatoes flavoured with mustard.

SERVES 4

apple and chutney sausages

8 sausages
1/2 cup sweet fruit chutney
1/2 cup finely chopped celery

567 g can apple slices
1 cup grated tasty cheddar cheese

Grill sausages or bake at 180ºC until cooked and golden brown.

Cut sausages lengthwise but do not cut right through. Spread with chutney and sprinkle with celery. Arrange apple slices on top and sprinkle with grated cheese. Return to oven and cook for about 10 minutes until apple is heated through and cheese has melted.

SERVES 4

sausage sizzler

Cook sausages on a grill tray in the oven to avoid cooking them in their own fat. Alternatively, drain off excess fat in the pan as the sausages cook.

crumbed sausages

1 cup Edmonds standard grade
   flour
2 eggs, beaten
1 cup fresh breadcrumbs
8–12 sausages
1 tablespoon oil

1/2 cup tomato sauce
1/2 cup soy sauce
1/2 cup brown sugar
juice of 1/2 a lemon
2 cloves garlic, crushed

Place flour, beaten eggs and breadcrumbs in three shallow bowls. Dip sausages first into flour, then into egg, and then coat evenly with breadcrumbs.

Heat oil in a roasting pan on the element and place sausages in it. Cook for 2–3 minutes, browning all over. Bake in oven at 200ºC for 15 minutes or until golden brown.

Combine tomato sauce, soy sauce, brown sugar, lemon juice and garlic in a jug or bowl. Pour over sausages and return to oven for a further 5–8 minutes or until sauce has thickened. Serve immediately with mashed potato and salad.

SERVES 4

sausages with beans and bacon

8–12 sausages
2 tablespoons oil
1 onion, finely sliced
2 cloves garlic, chopped
6 rashers rindless bacon, diced

400 g can baked beans
1 teaspoon curry powder
1 cup grated tasty cheese
salt and freshly ground
   black pepper

Lay sausages in a large roasting pan. Prick each a couple of times with a fork. Bake at 180ºC for 15 minutes. Drain off excess fat. Heat oil in a frying pan and cook onion and garlic until softened. Add bacon and cook for about 6 minutes or until crispy. Mix in beans and curry powder and heat through.

Pour bean and bacon mixture over sausages. Top with cheese. Sprinkle with salt and pepper. Bake at 180ºC for 15 minutes until cheese has melted and turned golden brown.

SERVES 4

5 things you probably didn't know about sausages

1. To reduce the fat in a sausage, it can be cooked in many ways. Boiling it first can reduce the amount of fat but also the flavour. Try grilling in an oven on a grill rack with a tray underneath. Try not to let sausages cook in the fat that naturally holds them together. The better quality the sausage, the less fat it will have in it, so spend slightly more to get decent sausages — it will be well worth it.

2. Sausages will burst if cooked at too high a temperature. Fry or bake them gently for 10 minutes, turning frequently until they are golden brown.

3. There is very little difference between a sausage, a frankfurter and a wiener. A frankfurter is named after its town of origin, Frankfurt; a wiener is so named because it comes from Wien (i.e. Vienna). Hot dogs got their name because a cartoonist once drew a head, tail and legs on a frankfurter to make it look like a dachshund.

4. A saveloy is made from smoked pork and the name comes from the French, 'cervelas'.

5. Sausages are best when cooked on the barbecue. Avoid cooking them from frozen, and if possible, pre-cook them by boiling in water for about 5 minutes or microwaving on High (100%) for 2–3 minutes. This will prevent the outer casing from burning before the inside is cooked.

roast chicken with lemon and rice stuffing
top right
PAGE **83**

marinated chicken wings
middle
PAGE **79**

thai chicken salad
below left
PAGE **81**

fish and shellfish

Fish and shellfish, more than any other food, are best when they are as fresh as they can possibly be. However, when fish or shellfish such as prawns and shrimps are snap-frozen, they are of an even better quality than some raw and straight-out-of-the-water catches. Snap-freezing is done at very low temperatures, while the vessels are still at sea, and most often on the same day as the fish is caught.

When buying fish, look for signs of freshness, such as: no smell of ammonia or other strong odour; the flesh is translucent and firm; the scales are intact; the gills are bright red; the eyes are bright and bulging; and there is no blood in the body cavity.

It is very important to handle fish and seafood carefully. If you have bought your fish filleted from a fish shop, it will need very little preparation. Keep the raw fish fillets well wrapped on the bottom shelf of the fridge to avoid liquid dripping from the fish onto other raw or cooked foods. Always keep raw fish cold as it will deteriorate rapidly at temperatures over 4°C.

Guide times for cooking fish depend on the size and thickness of the fish. Fish is cooked when the flesh flakes easily, or when the flesh separates from the bones, or when a creamy white juice comes from the flesh.

When in season, shellfish provide an inexpensive and plentiful source of food in this country. Mussels, cockles, oysters and scallops supply a great amount of natural oils and minerals, otherwise not found in our diet.

how to debeard a mussel . . . and other fishy tips

Removing scales — Remove the scales by first holding the fish under running cold water. Then, using a shell or small utensil, scrape firmly down the length of the fish from the tail end towards the head.

Freezing fish — Freeze extra fish fillets individually on a tray then place in labelled freezer bags for storage. This way you won't need to thaw the whole bag for just one fillet. Resist the temptation to freeze live mussels or cockles — it won't work.

Buying — Check when buying shellfish that they look plump and juicy, that they do not have a strong smell, that the shells do not remain open when tapped and that they have been stored correctly. Buy small amounts of shellfish, often, and store only for one or two days and no longer.

Removing bones — Use tweezers to remove any bones from larger fillets such as salmon, hapuka or snapper. Run your hand along the top part of the fillet, finding each bone and then gently pull it out with small tweezers.

Debearding mussels — Remove any beards or barnacles from the mussels just before cooking, as the mussels will die once the beards are gone. Use a small blunt knife or spoon and lever the beards away from the shell.

Deveining prawns — To devein large prawns before cooking, cut along the back of each shell. Remove the shell. The small dark vein runs along the back of the prawn. Make a small incision with a knife and remove this vein. Rinse prawn well under cold running water.

Preparing a whole fish — Make sure the fish has been gutted and cleaned before cooking it. Trim the fins and tail with kitchen scissors to prevent them from curling up and burning. Remove the head if desired. Simply cut it off, using a sharp knife, following the natural curve behind the gills.

To remove fishy smells — Rub the cut surface of a lemon over hands, knife and cutting board after preparing fish to counteract fishy odours.

creamy salmon filo pie

1 tablespoon oil
2 stalks celery, diced
1 leek, finely chopped
2 cups cooked white rice
2 teaspoons chopped, fresh dill
1 tablespoon lemon juice
2 1/2 cups White Sauce
   (see page 27)

1/2 teaspoon nutmeg
2 x 210 g cans pink salmon
salt and freshly ground
   black pepper
2 tablespoons butter, melted
8 sheets Edmonds filo pastry

Heat oil in a large frying pan. Cook celery and leek for about 3 minutes or until softened. Place in a bowl with rice, dill, lemon juice, white sauce and nutmeg. Mix well. Drain salmon and remove any bones and skin. Flake salmon into rice mixture and mix lightly. Do not break up salmon too much. Season to taste with salt and pepper.

Grease an ovenproof dish with melted butter. Layer filo pastry in dish, carefully brushing all sheets with melted butter. Spoon salmon mixture into pastry. Fold sides of pastry loosely over the top of salmon mixture. Bake in 200ºC oven for 15–20 minutes or until pastry is golden brown. Serve immediately with crisp green salad.   SERVES 4

salmon steaks
with mustard and dill

4 salmon steaks
oil
1/2 cup Mayonnaise (see page 56)

1/2 teaspoon chopped fresh dill
1/2 teaspoon prepared mustard

Brush salmon steaks with oil. Grill for 10 minutes or until salmon is cooked through, turning once during cooking. While salmon is cooking, combine mayonnaise, dill and mustard.

Carefully remove skin and bones from salmon. Place salmon on serving plates. Serve with mustard and dill mayonnaise.   SERVES 4

salmon cakes with parsley sauce

450 g potatoes
210 g can pink salmon
2 tablespoons butter
4 spring onions, chopped
1 tablespoon lemon juice
1 tablespoon chopped parsley
1 cup Edmonds standard grade
   flour

salt and freshly ground
   black pepper
1 egg, beaten
1 cup fresh white breadcrumbs
2 tablespoons oil
1 cup Parsley Sauce (see page 28),
   to serve

Peel potatoes, cut into evenly-sized pieces and cook in boiling salted water until tender. Drain well and mash until smooth. Drain salmon and flake, removing any skin and bones. Mix fish with potato. Melt butter in a small saucepan. Add spring onions and cook until they begin to soften. Add to fish mixture with lemon juice, parsley and flour. Season to taste with salt and pepper. Add just enough beaten egg to bind mixture. It must be firm enough to shape into cakes. With floured hands, shape mixture into 8 cakes. Brush with beaten egg and coat in breadcrumbs. Chill for 30 minutes. Heat oil in a frying pan and shallow-fry fish cakes (in batches, if necessary) for about 5 minutes on each side until golden and crisp. Drain on kitchen paper. Serve immediately with Parsley Sauce. **SERVES 4**

curried salmon slice

2 tablespoons oil
2 cloves garlic, crushed
1 onion, chopped
3 teaspoons mild curry powder
3/4 cup short grain rice
4 tomatoes, peeled and chopped
   (see page 107)
1 1/4 cups water

415 g can pink salmon, drained and
   flaked
1 tablespoon lemon juice
1 teaspoon grated lemon rind
2 cups grated tasty cheddar cheese
2 cups cornflakes, crushed
salad to serve
lemon slices to garnish

Lightly grease a 20 cm x 30 cm cake tin, and line base and sides with non-stick baking paper. Heat oil in a large pan, cook garlic and onion until onion is soft. Stir in curry powder and rice; stir over heat for 1 minute. Add tomatoes, water, salmon, lemon juice and rind. Bring to boil and then simmer, stirring for 5 minutes. Remove from heat, cool for 5 minutes. Stir in cheese. Pour into prepared pan, sprinkle with cornflakes. Cook in oven at 180ºC for 20 minutes. Cover with foil and cook for a further 30 minutes. Stand for 5 minutes before cutting into squares. Serve slices with salad, garnished with lemon slices. **SERVES 4**

tuna burgers

210 g can tuna in spring water
1 cup mashed potato
1 small onion, finely chopped
1/2 cup Edmonds standard grade
  flour
2 teaspoons Edmonds baking
  powder
salt and freshly ground black pepper
1/4 cup chopped parsley
1 egg, beaten

1 cup wholemeal breadcrumbs
oil for shallow frying

8 wholemeal burger buns or baps
alfalfa sprouts
tomato and cucumber slices
lettuce leaves
Mayonnaise (see page 56)

✍ Drain and flake the tuna, reserving the liquid. Combine tuna, reserved liquid, mashed potato and onion. Sieve flour and baking powder together into tuna mixture. Season with salt and pepper to taste. Add parsley. Mix well to combine.

Divide mixture into eight even-sized portions. Shape into rounds. Dip each burger into the beaten egg and then in the breadcrumbs to coat. Heat oil in a large frying pan. Cook burger patties until golden on both sides. Drain on absorbent paper.

Toast split burger buns or baps in the oven. Use one patty per bun and top with your choice of topping.   **SERVES 4**

tuna surprise

500 g spaghetti
2 tablespoons oil
1 onion, finely sliced
1 tablespoon curry powder
1 green capsicum, deseeded and
  sliced
450 g broccoli, cut into small florets

2 stalks celery, sliced
2 teaspoons powdered chicken
  stock
2 x 185 g cans tuna
salt and freshly ground
  black pepper

✍ Cook spaghetti according to instructions on packet. Drain.

Heat oil in a large frying pan. Add onion and curry powder and cook for 5 minutes. Add the capsicum, broccoli and celery and cook for another 3 minutes. Sprinkle over the chicken stock and 2 tablespoons of water. Cover the pan for 5 minutes to allow the vegetables to steam.

Drain the tuna and remove any skin and bones. Flake the fish and add to the vegetables. Toss lightly with a fork. Season with salt and pepper. Remove from heat and toss through the cooked spaghetti. Serve immediately or allow to cool and serve as a salad.   **SERVES 4**

tuna sauce with pasta

1 tablespoon oil
1 onion, chopped
2 x 400 g cans tomatoes in juice
2 tablespoons tomato paste
1/2 cup water
185 g can tuna in brine, drained
and roughly flaked

2 tablespoons chopped parsley
salt and freshly ground black
pepper
400 g pasta shapes, e.g. gnocchi

Heat oil in frying pan. Cook onion for 5 minutes until soft. Add tomatoes in juice, tomato paste and water, breaking up tomatoes with a wooden spoon. Simmer for 15–20 minutes until sauce is thick.

Stir in tuna and parsley. Season to taste. While sauce is cooking, cook pasta according to instructions on packet. Drain. Toss tuna sauce through pasta.

SERVES 4

tuna rice bake

3/4 cup long grain rice
2 tablespoons butter
1 clove garlic, crushed
1 onion, sliced
2 stalks celery, sliced
1 tablespoon Edmonds standard
grade flour
1 cup milk

2 eggs, beaten
1 1/2 cups grated tasty cheddar
cheese
2 tablespoons chopped parsley
425 g can tuna, drained and flaked
salt and freshly ground
black pepper

Place rice in a sieve. Wash under cold running water to remove starch. Cook rice in boiling water for 12 minutes until tender. Transfer to a sieve. Rinse under cold running water to cool. Drain thoroughly.

Melt butter in a saucepan. Add garlic, onion and celery. Cook for 5 minutes until onion is soft. Add flour and stir constantly for 2 minutes. Remove from heat. Gradually add milk, stirring constantly. Return pan to heat, stirring continuously, until sauce thickens and comes to the boil. Remove from heat.

Add eggs and half the cheese. Mix well. Stir in cooked rice, then parsley and tuna. Season to taste. Transfer mixture to a greased ovenproof dish. Sprinkle with remaining cheese. Cook at 180°C for 20 minutes or until golden. Serve hot or cold.

SERVES 4

5 things to do
with a can of tuna

Never underestimate the usefulness of a can of tuna in the pantry! A can of tuna will help you make quick and tasty meals in a matter of minutes. Here are some ideas.

- **Tuna Melt Pasta:** Cook pasta shapes and add some sliced leeks for the last 4 minutes of cooking. Drain well, then toss with 185 g flaked tuna, 1 cup grated tasty cheddar cheese, 1 tablespoon crème fraîche and salt and pepper.

- **Tuna and Couscous:** Soak 200 g of couscous until light and fluffy. Add a can of tuna, spring onions, cherry tomatoes and slices of cucumber. Mix together with a fork and pour over a ready-made vinaigrette.

- **American-style Sandwich:** Flake drained tuna with a few spoonfuls of mayonnaise mixed with some chopped gherkins, lemon juice and black pepper. Use to fill bagels or pita bread.

- **Tuna Potatoes:** Pile drained tuna chunks onto a halved baked potato and top with sour cream. Scatter over snipped chives and a good grinding of black pepper.

- **Seafood Pizza:** Spread a pizza base with pesto sauce and top with flaked tuna, chopped tomatoes, chopped spring onions, crumbled feta, a few pitted black olives, salt and pepper and a drizzle of olive oil. Bake in oven at 200°C for 15 minutes.

garlic prawns

pinch salt
2 large garlic cloves, roughly
    chopped
100 g butter, softened
1 teaspoon lemon juice

24 large cooked prawns, in their
    shells
salt and freshly ground
    black pepper
1 tablespoon chopped parsley

Add salt to garlic. Crush to a paste with the back of a knife. Mix with butter and lemon juice.

Melt 1/4 of the garlic butter in a large frying pan. Add prawns and fry gently for 2 minutes or until heated through. Season to taste with salt and pepper.

Stir parsley into remaining garlic butter. Add to frying pan and cook until hot and foaming. Spoon prawns and butter onto four warm serving plates.

SERVES 4

Tip: The garlic butter can be made ahead of time. Make double quantities and lay the remainder on a piece of greaseproof paper. Roll up into a cylinder and chill or freeze. Slice into rounds and use for more prawns, on bread, or with other fish dishes.

marinated raw fish

500 g firm white fish fillets, e.g.
    snapper, John Dory, tarakihi,
    gurnard
1 teaspoon salt
1/4 cup lemon juice

1 medium onion, finely chopped
1/2 cup coconut milk
2 tomatoes, diced
1/2 cup chopped cucumber

Cut fish into bite-sized pieces. Sprinkle with salt, then lemon juice. Cover and chill for 2 hours or until fish whitens, stirring occasionally. Drain. Stir in onion and coconut milk. Sprinkle tomatoes and cucumber over. Serve chilled.

SERVES 4–6

steamed **mussels**

1.5 kg fresh mussels	1 bay leaf
2 tablespoons oil	2 tablespoons fresh oregano,
25 g butter	chopped
1 onion, chopped	1 cup dry white wine
2 garlic cloves, crushed	

Scrub mussels in a sink of cold water. Discard any that float or are broken or remain open when tapped. Scrape off barnacles and remove beards. Place mussels in a clean bowl. Cover with cold water and swirl to remove grit or sand.

Melt oil and butter in a large saucepan. Add onion and garlic and cook for 5 minutes. Stir in bay leaf, oregano and wine. Bring to the boil. Add mussels, cover and cook for 5 minutes, shaking saucepan, until majority of mussels open. Discard any that remain closed. Transfer remaining mussels into a warmed bowl. Cover to keep warm. Serve with crusty bread. **SERVES 6**

mussels with bacon and mushroom

48 fresh live mussels	2 teaspoons crushed garlic
1 tablespoon oil	1 cup dry white wine
2 tablespoons butter	$3/4$ cup cream
1 onion, finely chopped	freshly ground black pepper
6 rashers bacon, diced	fresh parsley, to garnish
100 g button mushrooms, sliced	

Scrub the mussels in a sink of cold water. Discard any that float or are broken or remain open when tapped. Use a small knife to scrape off any barnacles, then pull off the wiry 'beards'. Put the cleaned mussels into a clean bowl. Pour cold water into the bowl and swirl the mussels round to get rid of any grit or sand.

Melt oil and half the butter in a large saucepan. Add onion, bacon, mushrooms and garlic and cook for 5 minutes. Stir in wine. Bring to the boil. Add mussels, cover and cook for 5 minutes, shaking saucepan, until majority of mussels open. Discard any that remain closed. Transfer remaining mussels and bacon into a warmed bowl. Cover to keep warm.

Simmer the liquid for 20 minutes or until reduced by half. Stir in cream, remaining butter and pepper. Return mussels and bacon to sauce and garnish with fresh parsley. Serve with crusty bread. **SERVES 4**

smoked fish and potato chowder

60 g butter
2 spring onions, chopped
1/3 cup Edmonds standard grade
   flour
pinch cayenne pepper
1/4 teaspoon salt
1/8 teaspoon freshly ground black
   pepper
450 g can smoked fish fillets

2 cups fish stock
410 g can whole-kernel corn,
   drained
2 potatoes, cubed
125 g frozen peeled prawns,
   thawed
2/3 cup sour cream
chopped parsley, to garnish

〜 Melt butter in a frying pan. Add spring onions and fry until softened. Stir in flour, cayenne pepper, salt and pepper. Cook for 1 minute.

Drain juice from smoked fish and set aside. Gradually add stock and reserved smoked fish juice to frying pan and bring to the boil. Add fish, corn and potatoes and simmer for 30 minutes or until potatoes are soft but still hold their shape. Add prawns and cook for a further 5 minutes.

Stir in sour cream. Sprinkle with parsley, then serve.   **SERVES 4**

easy seafood tortilla

16 cooked mussels, roughly
   chopped
1 cup cooked shrimps, chopped
2 spring onions, finely sliced
1 teaspoon grated root ginger
2 tablespoons sweet chilli sauce
salt and freshly ground
   black pepper

2 cups Edmonds standard grade
   flour
1 teaspoon Edmonds baking
   powder
1 cup soda water
2 tablespoons oil

〜 In a large bowl, mix together the mussels, shrimps, spring onions, ginger and sweet chilli sauce. Season to taste with salt and black pepper. Sift the flour and baking powder and add to the seafood mix. Mix in the soda water until the mixture is just combined. Do not over-mix. Heat the oil in a medium, non-stick frying pan. Spoon half the seafood mixture into the pan and spread it around the pan, making it into a full circle. Cook for about 6 minutes on one side, then carefully flip over using a spatula. Cook until golden brown on both sides.

Remove from the pan, drain on kitchen paper and keep warm. Repeat with the second half of the mixture. Cut the tortillas into eighths. Serve immediately with salad and sweet chilli sauce.   **SERVES 4**

steamed fish with lemon sauce

500 g skinned and boned fish fillets
2 tablespoons Edmonds Fielder's
   cornflour
1 cup chicken stock
1 teaspoon grated lemon rind

3 tablespoons lemon juice
1 egg
salt and freshly ground
   black pepper

Place fish fillets in a shallow microwave-proof dish, overlapping thin ends of fillets. Cover. Cook on High (100%) for 4–5 minutes, until fish is just cooked.

In a 2-cup microwave-proof jug, combine cornflour and stock. Cook on High for 2–2¹/₂ minutes, stirring once, until mixture thickens.

Place lemon rind in a 2-cup microwave-proof jug with the lemon juice and the egg. Beat to combine. Pour hot stock into lemon mixture, beating constantly. Heat on High for 1–1¹/₂ minutes. Stir and season to taste. Pour over fish.

SERVES 4

panfried fish with paprika

¹/₂ cup Edmonds standard grade
   flour
1 teaspoon paprika
salt and freshly ground
   black pepper
4 fillets firm white fish, e.g.
   tarakihi, snapper, gurnard

2 tablespoons butter
2 tablespoons oil
juice of 1 lemon
lemon wedges for garnish

Combine flour, paprika and salt and pepper to taste. Coat the fish fillets with the seasoned flour. Heat butter and oil in a frying pan. Place fish in pan and squeeze over the lemon juice.

Cook for 5 minutes on each side or until golden. Garnish with lemon wedges and serve with fresh vegetables.

SERVES 4

fresh as . . .

Keep fish and seafood refrigerated and well covered until ready to use. Do not store fish for more than 2-3 days — it is better to cook it immediately.

crunchy-topped fish pie

1 kg potatoes, cut into chunks
900 g white fish fillets, e.g. tarakihi,
   snapper or cod
2 cups milk
1 bay leaf
50 g butter, plus extra
1 onion, chopped

50 g Edmonds standard
   grade flour
1 cup cream
175 g large shrimps
25 g fresh dill, finely chopped
1$^1/_2$ cups grated tasty
   cheddar cheese

Parboil the potatoes for 8–10 minutes or until just tender. Drain well and set aside. Meanwhile, put the fish pieces into a wide saucepan, pour over the milk and add the bay leaf. Bring to the boil, then simmer for 3 minutes. Cover and remove from the heat. Leave to stand for 5 minutes or until the fish is just cooked. Remove the fish using a slotted spoon. Strain and reserve the cooking liquid for the sauce.

Lightly grease a 2-litre ovenproof dish. Flake the fish into large chunks, removing any skin and bones, and put in the dish.

Melt the butter in a pan, add the onion and fry for 3 minutes or until softened but not browned. Stir in the flour and cook for 1 minute. Remove the pan from the heat and slowly stir in the reserved cooking liquid and the cream. Return to the heat and cook, stirring until thickened, smooth and just boiling. Remove from the heat and stir in the shrimps and dill. Season with salt and pepper, then pour over the fish.

Toss a knob of butter with the potatoes along with 1 cup of the cheese, and season. Be careful not to break up the potatoes. Scatter the potatoes over the sauce so it is well covered. Sprinkle over the remaining cheese. Bake in oven at 200ºC for about 30 minutes or until the potatoes are golden. **SERVES 4–6**

baked lemon and sage fish

1 whole fish, about 1 kg in weight
1 teaspoon grated lemon rind
$^1/_4$ cup lemon juice
2 tablespoons melted butter

2 tablespoons chopped fresh sage
$^1/_2$ teaspoon salt
freshly ground black pepper

Remove scales from fish by running the back of a knife along the skin of the fish. Wash and dry fish. Cut 4 slashes in the top and bottom of the fish.

Mix lemon rind, lemon juice, melted butter, sage, salt and pepper together. Brush over skin, into slashes and inside body cavity of fish.

Wrap in a layer of baking paper then a layer of foil. Bake at 190ºC for 20–25 minutes or until fish flakes easily. **SERVES 4**

creamy salmon filo pie
top right

PAGE 93

salmon cakes with parsley sauce
middle

PAGE 94

salmon steaks with mustard and dill
below right

PAGE 93

garlic prawns
top left
PAGE 98

marinated raw fish
middle right
PAGE 98

easy seafood tortilla
below
PAGE 100

vegetarian
dishes

The natural flavours and colours of vegetables make for exciting meals-with-a-difference. Whether it is your choice to eliminate meat from your diet or whether you just feel a need to eat something new — vegetarian meals offer a great change from the meat-and-three-veges scenario.

It is better to under-cook rather than over-cook most vegetables. Resist the temptation to leave vegetables stewing or boiling on a stove for a long time. Sort out your cooking times before you start your meal. The longer you leave vegetables cooking, the more nutrients and minerals are sapped out of them.

Make the most of seasonal vegetables and fruit. They will be less expensive as well as being of much better quality. If you have an abundance of some vegetables in a particular season, try parboiling and freezing them to use later on.

Experiment with new and exciting vegetables. Asian greens and unusual varieties are being introduced to us all the time. Make the most of these new varieties to make your mealtimes different.

bean there, done that — lentils, beans and other pulses

Lentils and pulses are inexpensive, natural foods that offer many benefits for the cook. Pulses are the edible seeds of any legume such as beans, peas or lentils. They can be dried or fresh.

They are:
- rich in natural proteins that a lot of other vegetables don't have;
- inexpensive and easy to store;
- able to take on other flavours very well to create substantial and tasty meals.

With a little forward planning they can make any meal a less expensive and more creative option.

Most pulses need to be soaked in cold water for at least 4-8 hours. Alternatively, soak in boiling water for about 1 hour.

As a rule of thumb, the following are cooking times for some of the more common types of lentils and beans:
- split lentils — 15-20 minutes;
- whole lentils — 25-30 minutes;
- black-eyed beans — 45 minutes;
- black beans, cannellini beans, red kidney beans — about 1 hour;
- chickpeas, dried butter beans — 1¼ hours;
- dried broad beans, haricot beans — 1½ hours.

Season the beans and lentils towards the end of the cooking time since salt can prevent the softening process.

Always ensure that dried beans are cooked properly, as some can cause stomach upsets if under-cooked.

A quick dip can be made by mashing cooked and drained butter beans or chickpeas with a little chilli paste, olive oil and crushed garlic.

filo parcels with pumpkin and corn

700 g butternut pumpkin or squash
1 vegetable stock cube
2 tablespoons butter
salt and freshly ground
    black pepper
440 g can creamed corn

1 teaspoon curry powder
1/4 teaspoon cayenne pepper
12 sheets Edmonds filo pastry
melted butter, for brushing
sesame seeds

Peel and dice the pumpkin or squash. Cook until tender in a pot of boiling salted water. Drain, and crumble the vegetable stock cube over the pumpkin. Mash with the butter and season to taste. Stir in the creamed corn, curry powder and cayenne pepper.

Lay 3 sheets of filo pastry one on top of another, on a dry bench-top, and brush well with the melted butter. Spoon one quarter of the pumpkin mixture onto the middle of the sheets. Fold the edges up into a parcel and brush all over with more butter. Repeat with the other sheets of filo and the rest of the pumpkin mixture.

Place on a greased oven tray. Bake at 200ºC for 20–25 minutes, until pastry is golden brown and crispy. Serve immediately.   **SERVES 4**

spicy bean nacho pie

1 tablespoon olive oil
1 large onion, cut into wedges
1 large garlic clove, sliced
1 teaspoon ground coriander
2 tablespoons chopped fresh
    coriander
1 teaspoon ground cumin
1 teaspoon crushed dried chillies
1 teaspoon sugar

400 g can whole peeled tomatoes
1 chicken or vegetable stock cube
2 x 300 g cans mixed beans,
    drained
60 g tortilla chips
3/4 cup grated tasty cheddar cheese
salt and freshly ground
    black pepper
2 tablespoons sour cream

Heat oil in a frying pan. Fry onion for 5 minutes. Stir in garlic, ground and fresh coriander, cumin, chillies, sugar and tomatoes. Crumble in stock cube. Stir in beans and simmer for 10 minutes.

Preheat grill to high. Transfer mixture to an ovenproof dish. Scatter with tortilla chips and cheese. Season to taste with salt and pepper. Grill until cheese melts. Serve with sour cream.   **SERVES 2**

stir-fried vegetables
with noodles

2 tablespoons olive oil
1 tablespoon chopped parsley
1 egg, beaten
250 g egg noodles
2 cloves garlic, finely chopped
5-cm piece root ginger, cut into
  sticks

2 carrots, cut into sticks
125 g button mushrooms, sliced
125 g sugar-snap peas
200 g leeks, sliced
2 tablespoons hoisin sauce
150 ml vegetable stock

Heat half of the oil in a large frying pan. Mix the parsley and egg and pour into the pan to make a thin omelette. Cook for 1 minute on each side, then remove and put on a plate. Cook the noodles according to the instructions on the packet.

Heat the remaining oil in the pan. Add the garlic and ginger and stir-fry for 30 seconds. Add carrots and mushrooms and fry over a high heat for a few minutes, stirring occasionally. Add the peas and leeks and stir-fry for 2 minutes; season.

Pour in the hoisin sauce and stock and cook over a high heat for about 1 minute. Cut the omelette into thin strips. Drain the noodles, fork onto serving plates and top with the vegetables in their juices; pile the omelette strips on top.

SERVES 4

spicy squash stew

2 tablespoons olive oil
1 onion, chopped
1 garlic clove, finely chopped
450 g potatoes, roughly chopped
2 tablespoons curry powder
600 ml vegetable stock
450 g squash, roughly chopped
400 g can red kidney beans,

drained
$1/2$ teaspoon salt
$1/8$ teaspoon ground pepper
2 tablespoons chopped fresh
  coriander, to garnish
lemon wedges, to serve

Heat oil in a frying pan. Fry onion and garlic for 2 minutes until softened. Add potatoes and cook, stirring, for 3 minutes. Stir in curry powder. Add stock and bring to the boil. Simmer for 5 minutes.

Add squash. Cover and simmer for a further 15 minutes until vegetables are cooked. Add beans, salt and pepper. Cook until beans are warmed through.

Divide stew among serving plates or large shallow bowls. Sprinkle with coriander. Garnish with lemon wedges and serve with naan bread. SERVES 4

ratatouille

1/4 cup olive oil
6 medium tomatoes, blanched and
   chopped
1/2 teaspoon salt
freshly ground black pepper
1/4 teaspoon sugar

1 large onion, sliced
2 cloves garlic, crushed
1 green capsicum, deseeded
   and sliced
250 g courgettes, sliced
1 eggplant, chopped

Heat half the oil in a small saucepan. Add tomatoes, salt, pepper to taste, and sugar. Cook for 10 minutes or until mixture achieves sauce consistency, stirring frequently.

Heat remaining oil in a large frying pan or saucepan. Add onion and garlic and cook until onion is clear. Stir in capsicum, courgettes and eggplant.

Cover and cook slowly until vegetables are tender, stirring frequently. Add tomato mixture to the vegetables. Stir to combine. Serve hot.   **SERVES 4**

tasty potato and carrot layer

4 potatoes
1 onion
3 carrots
1/2 cup hot chicken stock

1 tablespoon butter
1 tablespoon finely chopped
   parsley

Peel and thinly slice potatoes and onion. Peel and coarsely grate carrots. In a microwave-proof dish, place a single layer of potato then a layer of carrot. Top with a layer of onion slices. Repeat until all vegetables are used, finishing with a layer of potato.

Add chicken stock. Dot with butter. Cover and cook in microwave on High (100%) for 14–16 minutes, or until vegetables are tender. Sprinkle with chopped parsley.   **SERVES 4**

skinny-dipping tomatoes

To skin tomatoes, place them in a bowl and pour over enough boiling water to cover. Leave for 30 seconds, then drain off water. Cool slightly before peeling off skins.

eggplant and tomato pie

3 medium eggplants, washed
salt
3 tablespoons Edmonds standard
    grade flour, seasoned with salt
    and pepper
6 tablespoons oil
125 g grated parmesan cheese

300 g jar pasta tomato sauce
a handful of fresh herbs
450 g mozzarella, sliced
salt and freshly ground
    black pepper
4 eggs, beaten
basil leaves, to garnish

Line a 20-cm-diameter cake tin with baking paper. Slice eggplants, place in a colander or large sieve, sprinkle with salt and allow to stand for 30 minutes.

Dry eggplant slices. Dip in seasoned flour. Heat 2 tablespoons of oil in a frying pan and fry in batches for 1 minute each side, adding oil as needed.

Sprinkle parmesan cheese in the bottom of the cake tin and lay 1/2 the eggplant slices on top. Layer with 1/2 the tomato sauce, 1/2 the herbs and 1/2 the mozzarella slices. Repeat with remaining ingredients. Season to taste with salt and pepper.

Make four small holes in the top layer. Pour beaten eggs over pie. Bake at 190ºC for 50 minutes. Let stand for 10 minutes. Turn out and cut into wedges. Garnish with basil and serve with a crisp salad.   **SERVES 6**

cheese and spinach bake

100 g butter, softened
1 1/2 tablespoons wholegrain
    mustard
10 thick slices white bread
1 tablespoon olive oil
1 large onion, chopped
3 cloves garlic
250 g spinach leaves

50 g grated parmesan cheese
1 3/4 cups grated tasty cheddar
    cheese
freshly ground black pepper
    to season
3 eggs, beaten
2 1/2 cups milk
1/2 teaspoon salt

Mix butter and mustard and use a little to grease a 30 x 20 cm ovenproof dish. Spread remaining mixture on both sides of bread. Cut bread into triangles.

Heat oil in a frying pan and fry onion gently for 6 minutes until soft and golden. Add garlic and spinach and fry for 3 minutes until spinach has wilted.

Arrange a layer of bread in the bottom of the dish and sprinkle with 1/2 spinach mixture and 1/3 parmesan and cheddar cheeses. Add another layer of bread, remaining spinach and another 1/3 of cheese. Top with remaining bread.

Sprinkle with remaining cheese and pepper. Mix eggs, milk and salt together. Pour over bread. Bake at 190ºC for 35 minutes until golden.   **SERVES 4**

microwaved
potato wedges

4 potatoes

1 onion

1/2 green capsicum

2 tablespoons butter

1 teaspoon chicken stock powder

1 tablespoon finely chopped parsley

1/2 cup grated tasty cheddar cheese

Scrub potatoes then grate. Do not peel. Rinse grated potatoes under cold water, drain thoroughly. Peel and finely chop onion. Deseed and finely chop capsicum.

Place butter in a microwave-proof bowl. Cover. Melt on High (100%) for 40–50 seconds. Add chicken stock powder, parsley, potatoes, onion and green capsicum. Mix to combine. Press potato mixture into a microwave-proof ring mould.

Sprinkle with grated cheese. Cover and cook on High for 10–12 minutes or until potato is tender. Allow to stand for 2 minutes. Serve, cut into wedges.

SERVES 4

spicy cajun
potato wedges

3 tablespoons Edmonds standard grade flour

3 teaspoons Cajun spice mix

1/2 teaspoon chilli powder

6 medium potatoes, washed

oil to coat

sour cream to serve

paprika to garnish

Combine flour, Cajun spice mix and chilli powder. Place in a plastic bag. Cut potatoes in half lengthwise, then cut each half into 4 wedges. Place wedges in a bowl. Pour over just enough oil to lightly coat the potatoes once tossed thoroughly.

Transfer wedges to the plastic bag. Twist top of bag and shake vigorously to coat. Preheat oven to 220ºC, placing a large roasting pan in the oven to heat. Place wedges in heated roasting pan.

Bake for 40 minutes, turning occasionally, until potatoes are cooked through and golden. Accompany with sour cream that has been lightly sprinkled with paprika.

SERVES 4 AS A SNACK

broccoli with cheese sauce

2 heads broccoli
25 g butter
2 tablespoons Edmonds standard
    grade flour
2 cups milk

3/4 cup grated tasty cheese
salt and white pepper
1/2 teaspoon dry mustard
grated fresh parmesan to serve

✿ Cook broccoli in boiling salted water until tender (about 7 minutes). While broccoli is cooking, melt the butter in a saucepan. Stir in flour and cook until frothy. Gradually add milk, stirring constantly until mixture boils and thickens. Remove from heat. Add 1/2 cup of the cheese, salt and pepper to taste and mustard.

Drain broccoli and transfer to an ovenproof serving dish. Pour sauce over the broccoli. Sprinkle with remaining cheese. Cook at 190ºC for 10 minutes. Serve with fresh, grated parmesan sprinkled over the top. **SERVES 4**

new potatoes
with mint yoghurt

900 g baby new potatoes, scrubbed
250 g unsweetened yoghurt
6 sprigs mint leaves

1 tablespoon lemon juice

✿ Bring a pot of salted water to the boil. Cook potatoes for 18 minutes until tender. In the last 2 minutes, add 2–3 sprigs of the mint leaves. Drain well.

Finely slice the rest of the mint leaves, leaving a few for garnishing. In a small bowl or jug mix together the yoghurt, mint leaves and lemon juice. Pour over the potatoes and serve immediately. Garnish with additional mint leaves.

SERVES 4

scrubs up nicely

Keep a separate nailbrush for cleaning vegetables such as potatoes, kumara and carrots.

twice-baked **kumara**

2 large kumara
**¹/₄ cup unsweetened natural
  yoghurt**

¹/₂ teaspoon chilli powder
2 tablespoons butter

Scrub kumara and prick several times with a fork. Place on a paper towel and cook in microwave on High (100%) for 8–9 minutes, or until soft. Allow to stand for 5 minutes. Cut kumara in half lengthwise and scoop out flesh, leaving skin about 0.5 cm thick.

Place flesh in food processor with yoghurt, chilli powder and butter. Process until smooth. Alternatively, mash kumara and remaining ingredients together. Spoon mashed mixture back into kumara shells. Place on a microwave-proof plate and cook on High (100%) for 2–3 minutes to heat through. **SERVES 4**

beans with bacon

450 g long green beans, trimmed
1 tablespoon olive oil

1 red onion, finely diced
4 rashers streaky bacon, diced

Quickly cook the beans in a pot of boiling water for 3–4 minutes or until tender. In another small frying pan heat the oil.

Fry the onion for 5 minutes, then add the bacon. Tip out any excess fat that comes off the bacon. Toss the beans through the bacon and onion mixture. Serve immediately. **SERVES 4**

Tip: Serve this salad cold as an accompaniment to main meal dishes.

short rations

To save time when cutting up bacon, use a pair of kitchen scissors to snip away at the rashers. If your household doesn't have kitchen scissors, wash another pair of scissors thoroughly before and after using them.

glazed **carrots**

750 g carrots, peeled and sliced
1 tablespoon butter
1 tablespoon sesame seeds

1 tablespoon brown sugar
1 tablespoon golden syrup

◈ Boil carrots in salted water until tender. Drain. Melt butter in a pan and brown slightly. Add sesame seeds and cook for 2 minutes. Add brown sugar and golden syrup. Add the carrots to this, tossing them until they are glazed all over.

SERVES 4

---

sautéed **courgettes**

1 tablespoon oil
1 onion, sliced
2 cloves garlic, crushed
500 g courgettes, thinly sliced

$1/2$ teaspoon salt
freshly ground black pepper
1 teaspoon chicken stock powder
1 teaspoon poppy seeds

◈ Heat oil in a large saucepan. Add onion and garlic. Cook until onion is clear. Add courgettes, salt, and pepper to taste. Stir. Add chicken stock and poppy seeds. Cover and cook over a low heat until tender. **SERVES 4**

---

all wrapped up

Wrap any leftover vegetables from your evening meal in buttered tinfoil, adding some fresh herbs. The next meal time, simply put the tinfoil package in the oven to reheat. Alternatively, toss all the remaining vegetables together in a plastic container with some vinaigrette and take them with you the next day for a quick salad lunch.

new potatoes with mint yoghurt
top
PAGE 110

glazed carrots
middle left
PAGE 112

broccoli with cheese sauce
middle right
PAGE 110

beans with bacon
below left
PAGE 111

desserts

Whether as a sweet temptation to end a meal or just as a quick 'sugar fix', desserts are the delights of the kitchen. They are not difficult to make and they can round off a meal perfectly.

A special hot pudding or chilled dessert can make the most of any seasonal fruit. Use fruit when in abundance on the tree or vine. Alternatively, fill your cupboard with cans of fruit for quick desserts.

Desserts don't need to be too lavish or complex. Simple flavours such as chocolate or berry will work well. Choose your recipe to complement the main meal. A light lemon meringue pie will go down nicely after a salmon or chicken dish. Berries and stone fruits will round off a meal that started with a beef or lamb dish.

Use different plates or tall-stemmed glasses to serve crumbles and delicate creams. There is no need to rush out and buy crystal parfait glasses.

Low-fat options are often good. Use low-fat yoghurt or light cream instead of full fat. A cake or sponge can be heated quickly in the microwave or oven and served with ice-cream. A dollop of cream will provide the indulgent finish to any meal.

dessert sauces

chocolate sauce

1 tablespoon Edmonds Fielder's
  cornflour
1/4 cup cocoa

1 cup milk
1–2 tablespoons sugar
1 tablespoon butter

In a saucepan, mix cornflour, cocoa and 1/4 cup of the milk to a smooth paste. Add the remaining milk, sugar, butter and cook, stirring constantly for 2–3 minutes or until thick and smooth.

MAKES 1 CUP

caramel sauce

125 g butter
3/4 cup brown sugar
1 1/2 tablespoons Edmonds Fielder's
  cornflour

1 cup water
1 tablespoon golden syrup
1/2 cup cream

Melt butter and sugar in a saucepan, stirring constantly until sugar dissolves. Boil for 3 minutes, stirring occasionally. Remove from heat. In a bowl, combine cornflour, water and golden syrup until smooth. Add to saucepan. Bring mixture back to the boil, stirring constantly. Boil for 2 minutes. Remove from heat. Add cream.

MAKES ABOUT 2 CUPS

custard

1 tablespoon Edmonds custard
  powder
1 cup milk

1 egg, beaten
1 teaspoon sugar

In a saucepan, mix custard powder and 2 tablespoons of the milk to a smooth paste. Add the remaining milk, egg and sugar and cook, stirring constantly, until custard thickens. Do not boil.

MAKES 1 CUP

Tip: To make vanilla custard, add 1/2 teaspoon vanilla essence.

banana custard

1/4 cup sugar
1/4 cup Edmonds custard powder
2 cups milk
1 tablespoon butter

1 tablespoon cream
3–4 bananas
about 1 tablespoon lemon juice
whipped cream

Combine sugar and custard powder in a 2-litre microwave-proof jug. Gradually stir in milk. Cook on High (100%) for 4–5 minutes, stirring twice until custard boils and thickens. Stir in butter and cream. Peel bananas and slice into four individual serving dishes. Spoon lemon juice on top. Pour custard evenly over bananas. Cool, then refrigerate until cold. Serve with whipped cream.

SERVES 4

fruit kebabs

selection of seasonal fruit
marshmallows (optional)

8 bamboo skewers
whipped cream, to serve

❧ Cut fruit into bite-sized pieces. Thread fruit randomly onto each skewer, alternating with the marshmallows if desired. Serve with sweetened whipped cream or yoghurt.   **SERVES 4**

Variation
Soak the skewers in water for 30 minutes beforehand. Grill the fruit kebabs on a barbecue or grill plate as a warm dessert and serve with custard.

---

summer berry terrine

2 x 85 g packets raspberry
  jelly crystals
3¹/₂ cups sparkling wine
250 g raspberries

500 g strawberries, hulled
250 g blueberries
4–5 sprigs of fresh mint leaves
fresh berries to garnish

❧ In a large jug or bowl, mix the jelly crystals with 150 ml of boiling water and stir continuously until dissolved. Add the sparkling wine and stir well to combine.

In a terrine tin, jelly mould or loaf tin, put a layer of raspberries, strawberries and blueberries on the bottom, covering the whole base. Place a few mint leaves around the berries. Carefully pour 2.5 cm of the jelly over the berries. Place in the coldest part of the fridge and leave to set – this should take about 30 minutes.

When jelly has set, repeat with another layer of berries and mint leaves and cover again with another layer (2.5 cm) of jelly. Put back in the fridge until set. Repeat until the berries and jelly come up to the top of the mould, making up the second jelly packet with sparkling wine as required.

Leave to set overnight in the fridge. Place the whole tin in some warm water for a few seconds before turning it upside down. Remove the mould carefully. Serve on a platter topped with fresh berries.   **SERVES 6–8**

---

orange jelly whip

85 g packet orange jelly crystals
1 cup boiling water
1/2 cup cold water
2 bananas, mashed

300 ml thickened cream, whipped
   to soft peaks
orange slices
shredded orange rind (optional)

🍮 Put jelly crystals in a medium-sized heatproof bowl. Add boiling water and stir to dissolve. Add cold water and stir to combine. Chill until partially set. Using electric beater, beat until thick and fluffy.

Fold bananas and cream into jelly mix. Spoon into individual glasses. Refrigerate until firm. Just before serving, top with orange slices and rind if desired.

SERVES 6

---

caramel bananas

4 ripe bananas
juice of 1 lemon
4 tablespoons honey

2 tablespoons brown sugar
2 tablespoons butter

🍮 Peel and then cut bananas lengthways in half. Toss the bananas in the lemon juice. Heat the honey, brown sugar and butter in a small frying pan. Bring to a slow boil on a low heat. Put the bananas in the pan and continue to boil.

Turn once or twice to coat evenly. Cook for about 3–4 minutes. Serve with a scoop of ice-cream or whipped cream, pouring sauce over the top of the banana and ice-cream.

SERVES 4

easy **chocolate** mousse

150 g cooking chocolate
4 eggs, separated
300 ml cream
2 tablespoons sugar

cream to serve
grated chocolate to serve

❧ Break chocolate into the top of a double boiler. Stir over hot water until chocolate has melted. Allow to cool slightly. Stir yolks into chocolate. Beat until thick and smooth. Beat cream until thick. Quickly fold chocolate mixture into cream.

Beat egg whites until stiff but not dry. Gradually add sugar, beating until thick and glossy. Fold half of the egg-white mixture into chocolate mixture until well mixed. Repeat with remaining egg-white mixture. Pour into four or six individual dishes or one large one. Chill until firm. Serve decorated with whipped cream and chocolate. **SERVES 4−6**

Variation
- **Chocolate Liqueur Mousse** — Add 1 tablespoon brandy, chocolate or coffee liqueur to melted chocolate.

cheesecake

250 g packet digestive biscuits
1 teaspoon grated lemon rind
1 tablespoon lemon juice
75 g butter, melted

FILLING
2 teaspoons gelatine

2 tablespoons water
250 g pot cream cheese
250 g pot sour cream
1/2 cup sugar
2 tablespoons lemon juice
1 teaspoon lemon rind
1 teaspoon vanilla essence

❧ Finely crush biscuits. Combine biscuit crumbs, lemon rind, lemon juice and butter. Line the base and sides of a 20-cm spring-form tin with biscuit mixture. Chill while preparing filling. Pour filling into prepared base. Chill until set.

To make filling: Combine gelatine and water. Leave to swell for 10 minutes. Beat cream cheese until soft. Add sour cream and beat until well combined. Add sugar, lemon juice, lemon rind and vanilla. Beat until sugar has dissolved. Dissolve gelatine in a bowl placed over a saucepan of simmering water. Add to cheese mixture. **SERVES 6**

gingernut cheesecakes

150 g gingernut biscuits
500 g cream cheese
grated rind of 1 lemon
1/4 cup lemon juice

1/4 cup orange juice
1/2 cup caster sugar
lemon rind and fruit slices, to serve

Put the biscuits into a plastic bag, seal and lightly crush with a rolling pin. Divide the crumbs between 4 parfait glasses.

Put the cheese, lemon rind, lemon and orange juice and sugar in the large bowl of a food processor or mix with a wooden spoon until smooth. Spoon the mixture into the glasses and cover.

Chill for 1 hour until the cheese has set. Garnish with lemon rind and slices of fruit.

SERVES 4

---

lemon meringue pie

Edmonds sweet short pastry
   (or see recipe page 134,
   makes 200 g)

FILLING
5 tablespoons Edmonds Fielder's
   cornflour
1 cup sugar
2 teaspoons grated lemon zest

1/2 cup lemon juice
3/4 cup water
4 eggs, separated
1 tablespoon butter

TOPPING
1/4 cup caster sugar
1/4 teaspoon vanilla essence

On a lightly floured surface, roll out pastry to a 6-mm thickness. Use to line a 20-cm flan ring. Trim off any excess pastry. Bake blind at 190°C for 20 minutes (see page 22). Remove baking blind material. Return pastry shell to oven for 1 minute to dry out pastry base.

While pastry is cooking, make the filling. Blend cornflour, sugar, lemon zest and juice together until smooth. Add water. Cook over a medium heat until mixture boils and thickens, stirring constantly. Remove from heat. Stir in yolks and butter. Pour filling into cooked pastry base. Spoon meringue topping over lemon filling. To make the meringue, beat egg whites until stiff but not dry. Beat in sugar, 1 tablespoon at a time, until mixture is very thick and glossy. Stir in vanilla. Return pie to oven and bake at 190°C for 10 minutes or until golden.

SERVES 6

apple betty

1.5 kg dessert apples, such as
  granny smith or braeburn
2/3 cup orange juice
1 teaspoon vanilla essence
25 g butter
150 g fresh white breadcrumbs
110 g rolled oats

2 tablespoons chopped nuts, such
  as roasted peanuts and
  hazelnuts
2 tablespoons liquid honey
1/4 teaspoon cinnamon
yoghurt, to serve

  Peel, core and roughly chop the apples, then put them into a large, heavy-based pan with the orange juice and vanilla essence. Put the pan over a medium heat and bring mixture to the boil. Turn the heat down, cover the pan and cook apples until they begin to break down. Remove the lid and continue cooking until all the liquid has reduced and apples are a thick purée.

    In a large frying pan, melt the butter and add the breadcrumbs and oats. Stir until butter is well combined and the oats are toasted. Add the nuts and honey. In a 1.5-litre ovenproof dish layer the apple purée with the breadcrumb-and-oat mixture, finishing with an oat layer on top.

    Dust the top with cinnamon and bake in oven at 180ºC for 20 minutes. Serve warm with yoghurt.   **SERVES 6**

ambrosia

1½ cups cream
2 x 150 g pottles strawberry
  yoghurt
425 g can pears
425 g can peaches

180 g marshmallows
fresh blueberries, raspberries,
  strawberries or blackberries
toasted coconut threads, or
  desiccated coconut, to garnish

  Whip cream until it is double its original thickness. Fold cream and yoghurt together. Drain juice from pears and peaches. Slice canned fruit into bite-size pieces. Stir marshmallows and canned fruit into cream mixture. Pour into glasses and top with fresh fruit and coconut. Leave to chill for 30 minutes before serving.

SERVES 4–6

chocolate fudge
self-saucing pudding

50 g butter
1¹/₂ cups Edmonds standard
   grade flour
2 teaspoons Edmonds baking
   powder
1 cup caster sugar
3 tablespoons cocoa

¹/₃ cup milk
2 teaspoons vanilla essence
³/₄ cup brown sugar
5 tablespoons cocoa
2 cups boiling water

Melt butter in a medium-sized microwave-proof pudding bowl. Stir in flour, baking powder, sugar, first measure of cocoa, milk and vanilla. Do not overbeat. Mix brown sugar and second measure of cocoa together. Sprinkle over mixture in bowl.

Carefully pour the boiling water over. Cook in microwave, uncovered, on High (100%) for 12–14 minutes, until centre is just cooked. Allow to stand for 5 minutes before serving.

SERVES 4

---

baked sweet apricot cake

410 g can apricots in juice, drained
3 tablespoons sugar
300 g butter
1¹/₂ cups caster sugar
3 eggs
finely grated rind of 1 lemon

1 teaspoon vanilla essence
1 cup milk
3¹/₂ cups Edmonds high grade flour
1 teaspoon Edmonds baking
   powder

Grease a large lasagne dish. Lay apricots in the dish and sprinkle with a little of the sugar. In a large bowl, cream together butter and caster sugar until light and fluffy.

Add eggs, beating well after each addition. Add lemon rind and vanilla essence. Stir in milk, flour and baking powder.

Pour mixture over the top of the apricots. Bake at 180°C for 60–65 minutes. Serve warm with cream.

SERVES 6

bread and butter
pudding

4 x 2-cm-thick slices stale spiced
   fruit loaf or croissants
4 eggs
1 cup milk

$1/2$ cup cream
1 teaspoon grated lemon rind
icing sugar

୶ Cut bread or croissants into quarters and arrange to cover the base of an ovenproof dish. Beat eggs, milk, cream and lemon rind together until combined. Pour through a sieve over bread.

   Place dish in a roasting pan. Half-fill the roasting pan with boiling water and cover with foil. Bake at 180ºC for 30–35 minutes or until set. Serve dusted with icing sugar.

SERVES 6

Tip: Make use of stale bread; use any kind of bread such as baps, bread rolls or wholemeal loaves.

---

hot raisin and chocolate
sponge pudding

150 g dark chocolate
a little butter
$1/2$ cup caster sugar

4 eggs, separated
50 g raisins

୶ Break chocolate into small pieces and melt in a bowl placed over a saucepan of simmering water or microwave on Medium (75%) for $2^1/2$ minutes. Grease a 1-litre ovenproof pudding basin or bowl and sprinkle with a little of the sugar.

   In a large bowl, whisk the egg yolks and the remaining sugar together until they are creamy. Stir in the raisins.

   In another bowl, whisk the egg whites until stiff and peaked. Fold the melted chocolate into the egg yolks and sugar using a rubber spatula. Then fold in the egg whites. Do not over-mix. Spoon the mixture into the prepared dish.

   Bake in oven at 200ºC for 25–30 minutes. The pudding is cooked when it is spongy. Serve with cream.

SERVES 4

apple pie

200 g Edmonds sweet short pastry
  (or see recipe page 134)
2 teaspoons sugar
4–6 granny smith apples
1/2 cup sugar

25 g butter, melted
2 tablespoons Edmonds standard
  grade flour
1/4 teaspoon ground cloves

On a lightly floured surface, roll out pastry slightly larger than a 20-cm pie plate. Cut two 2.5-cm-wide strips long enough to go around the edge of the pie plate. Brush with water. Spoon apple filling into centre of pie plate.

To make the filling: Peel, core and slice apples thinly. Combine sugar, butter, flour and cloves. Toss apples in this mixture. Cover with remaining pastry. Press edges firmly together to seal. Cut steam holes in centre of pastry. Trim and crimp edges. Decorate pie with any pastry trimmings. Brush lightly with milk or water. Sprinkle with sugar.

Bake at 200ºC for 25 minutes or until pastry is golden. Test with a skewer to see if the apple is cooked. If not, reduce oven temperature to 180ºC and cook until apple is tender. **SERVES 6**

banoffee pie

100 g gingernut biscuits
100 g digestive biscuits
1 teaspoon mixed spice
230 g butter, softened
395 g can sweetened
  condensed milk

2 tablespoons cream
6 bananas
cocoa, to sprinkle
whipped cream, to serve

Place gingernuts and digestive biscuits in a plastic bag and crush finely with a rolling pin. Place in a bowl, stir in mixed spice and half the butter. Line an 18 to 20-cm-diameter flan or cake tin with plastic film. Use a spoon to press the biscuit mixture into the bottom of the tin. Chill to set. Place remaining butter in a saucepan, add condensed milk and bring to the boil, stirring constantly. Reduce the heat and simmer for 5–6 minutes, stirring slowly, until mixture is a light golden colour. Remove from the heat. Beat in 2 tablespoons cream and cool. Pour this caramel on top of biscuit base. Slice bananas and arrange on top of caramel. Sprinkle with cocoa. Chill. Serve topped with whipped cream and dusted with more cocoa.

SERVES 6–8

cakes and baking

The best thing about baking your own cakes — apart from having sweet treats always to hand — is that home baking is cheap! Buying flour and a few baking ingredients instead of commercial cakes and biscuits is a significant budget beater in the long run. It is also worth it for the therapeutic value and pride you can take in making your own cakes.

Having the right equipment helps. Invest a few dollars in a cake tin or two, some measuring spoons and cups and perhaps even a cake mixer, and your patisserie skills will come alive.

A good cake can be a visual feast — any design or icing ideas can turn your cakes into interesting gifts and surprises on a special day.

Essential tips for making cakes include:

1. Preheat the oven and prepare cake tins before starting to mix ingredients.
2. Sift dry ingredients when advised to do so in the recipe.
3. Fold sifted dry ingredients alternately with liquids — beginning and ending with dry ingredients. Do not beat. Mix just enough to combine the ingredients. Over-mixing produces a tough, low-volume cake.
4. To cream butter and sugar, use soft but not melted butter. Creaming beats air into the mixture which helps the cake to rise.
5. Mix ingredients more quickly by using a slotted spoon.
6. Leave cakes until completely cold before filling and icing them.

Making your own biscuits and slices will solve your lunch-box and snack worries. The less fuss the better! Remember to store your baking in airtight containers, and they will last for 2–3 weeks . . . if they haven't been devoured before then!

Baking bread and muffins doesn't take long and is a great cost-cutter in any flat. The smell of fresh baking will fill every room of the house and make Sunday brunch a pleasant time and one to look forward to for you and your flatmates.

hot tips for baking

Lining tins
- Line tins with baking paper or any extra butter paper. This helps prevent the cake sticking and also reduces cleaning-up time.
- Spray or brush oil onto the tin instead of using butter. Oil is less likely to burn or stick and is easier to use.

Baking
- When is a cake cooked? To test, insert a knife or skewer into the thickest part in the middle. If the knife comes out clean and with no moisture on it, then the cake is cooked. Another way to tell is to lightly apply pressure to the top of the cake with your fingertips. The top should feel firm and springy.
- If by chance your cake overcooks and becomes dry and unpalatable, pierce the top a few times with a skewer. Pour over rum, brandy, or whisky and leave for 24 hours. Alternatively, make a sugar syrup using lemon juice and sugar, or melt jam with a little hot water and pour over the cake.

Removing cakes from tins after baking
- Allow cake to stand in the tin for 3–5 minutes before turning out. This will help it firm up and it will come away from the sides a little.

Biscuits and cookies
- If there is no cookie cutter to be found, use the rim of an upturned wine glass to cut rounds from rolled-out cookie dough.
- Double the biscuit mixture when making. The extra mixture that you don't use can be rolled up in greaseproof paper and stored in the fridge for up to 2 weeks. Alternatively, freeze the dough in a roll, then cut off thin slices and bake, for instant biscuits.

wholemeal bread

1¹⁄₄ cups hot water
¹⁄₄ cup honey
³⁄₄ cup milk
1 tablespoon Edmonds active yeast

4 cups Edmonds wholemeal flour
2 cups Edmonds high grade flour
1¹⁄₂ teaspoons salt
50 g butter

❧ Combine hot water, honey and milk. Leave to cool until lukewarm. Sprinkle yeast over and leave for 10 minutes or until frothy. Combine 3 cups of the wholemeal flour, the high grade flour, and the salt in a bowl. Set remaining cup of wholemeal flour aside.

Cut in butter until mixture resembles coarse breadcrumbs. Make a well in the centre of the flour. Add frothy yeast mixture. Stir until well mixed. Turn out onto a lightly floured surface, using part of the reserved cup of flour for this. Knead the dough until it is smooth and elastic. If it is still sticky, add a little of the reserved flour, kneading until smooth or until dough springs back when lightly touched.

Lightly oil a bowl. Place dough in the bowl and brush lightly with oil. Cover and leave in a warm place until double in size. Punch dough down in the centre, then lightly knead. Divide dough in half. Shape into ovals. Place dough in two greased 22 x 13 cm loaf tins. Cover and leave until dough rises to top of tins. Bake at 200ºC for 40 minutes or until loaf sounds hollow when tapped on base of bread.

Tip: Make smaller loaves of bread by putting the dough mixture into small (new) terracotta flowerpots. The loaves can be removed and frozen for later use, and they look great for parties and special dinners.

corn, cheese and bacon muffins

2 rashers bacon, rind removed
2 cups Edmonds standard grade flour
5 teaspoons Edmonds baking powder

310 g can cream-style corn
2 eggs
1 cup milk
2 cups grated tasty cheddar cheese

❧ Chop bacon into small pieces. Fry lightly and drain. Sift flour and baking powder into a bowl. Make a well in the centre. Mix corn, eggs, bacon and milk together.

Pour corn mixture into dry ingredients and add half the cheese. Mix quickly until just combined. Three-quarters fill greased muffin tins with the mixture. Sprinkle with remaining cheese.

Bake at 190ºC for 20 minutes or until muffins spring back when lightly touched.

MAKES 12

cakes and
baking

blueberry **muffins**

3 cups Edmonds standard grade
    flour
5 teaspoons Edmonds baking
    powder
1/4 cup sugar

50 g butter
3 eggs
1 1/2 cups milk
2 cups blueberries, fresh or frozen
icing sugar

✍ Sift flour and baking powder into a bowl. Mix in sugar. Melt butter. Lightly beat eggs and milk together. Make a well in the centre of the dry ingredients.

Add butter, milk mixture and blueberries. Mix quickly until just combined. Three-quarters fill greased muffin tins with mixture. Bake at 200ºC for 15 minutes or until muffins spring back when lightly touched. Serve warm, dusted with icing sugar.

MAKES 12

chinese **chews**

2 eggs
1 cup brown sugar
75 g butter, melted
1 teaspoon vanilla essence
1 1/2 cups Edmonds standard
    grade flour
1 teaspoon Edmonds baking
    powder

pinch of salt
1/2 cup rolled oats
3/4 cup chopped dates
3/4 cup chopped walnuts
3/4 cup crystallised ginger

✍ Beat eggs and brown sugar until well mixed. Add butter and vanilla. Sift flour, baking powder and salt into a large bowl. Stir in rolled oats. Pour egg mixture into the sifted dry ingredients.

Add dates, walnuts and ginger. Mix well. Spread mixture into a 23-cm square cake tin lined on the base with baking paper.

Bake at 180ºC for 30–35 minutes or until cooked. Cut into squares while still hot.

MAKES 36 SQUARES

caramel date squares

FILLING
1 cup pitted dates, chopped
1 cup water
1 tablespoon brown sugar
1 teaspoon butter
2 teaspoons cocoa
1/4 teaspoon vanilla essence

BASE
125 g butter
1/2 cup sugar
1 egg
1 3/4 cups Edmonds standard
  grade flour
1 teaspoon Edmonds baking
  powder

To make the filling, combine dates, water, sugar, butter and cocoa in a saucepan. Cook gently over a low heat, stirring frequently, until a paste-like consistency is obtained. Add vanilla essence. Cool.

For the base, cream butter and sugar until light and fluffy. Add egg and beat well. Sift flour and baking powder together. Stir into creamed mixture.

Press out half the base mixture to fit the base of a greased 20-cm square tin. Spread with date mixture. Crumble remaining base mixture over filling. Press lightly with the back of a spoon.

Bake at 180°C for 30 minutes or until golden. Cut into fingers.

MAKES 25 SQUARES

Tip: Other dried fruits such as prunes, apricots and raisins, alone or mixed, can replace dates.

---

no-bake choc crunchies

100 g butter, plus a little extra for
  greasing
200 g digestive biscuits
3 tablespoons golden syrup

2 tablespoons cocoa
50 g raisins
100 g plain chocolate

Grease an 18-cm-diameter sandwich tin with butter. Seal biscuits in a strong polythene bag and break into uneven crumbs with a rolling pin.

Melt golden syrup and remaining 100 g of butter in a saucepan (or microwave on High (100%) for about 1 1/2 minutes). Stir in cocoa and raisins. Stir in biscuit crumbs thoroughly. Spoon into tin and press down firmly.

Melt chocolate in a heatproof bowl over a saucepan of simmering water (or microwave on Medium (75%) for 2 1/2 minutes). Spread over biscuit base and chill for about 30 minutes. Keeps for up to a week wrapped in foil. **MAKES 8–10**

rocky road slice

BASE
1 cup Edmonds standard grade
flour
1/2 teaspoon Edmonds baking
powder
3 tablespoons cocoa
3/4 cup caster sugar
3/4 cup coconut
125 g butter, melted
1 egg

TOPPING
250 g dark chocolate, chopped (or
melts, or bits)
2 tablespoons Kremelta
25 marshmallows
1/2 cup toasted coconut
1/2 cup pistachio nuts (or chopped
walnuts)

Sift flour, baking powder and cocoa into a bowl. Stir in caster sugar and coconut. Add butter and egg and mix well. Spread over the base of a greased 18 x 27 cm shallow baking tin. Bake at 180ºC for 20–25 minutes. Cool for 15 minutes, then spread with topping. To make the topping, place chocolate and Kremelta in a heatproof bowl. Place bowl over a saucepan of simmering water. Stir continuously until chocolate and Kremelta have melted and the mixture is smooth.

Set aside for 5 minutes to cool slightly. Add marshmallows, coconut and nuts to melted chocolate. Mix well. Spread over warm base. Allow topping to set before cutting into pieces. **MAKES 18 SLICES**

ginger crunch

125 g butter, softened
1/2 cup sugar
1 1/2 cups Edmonds standard
grade flour
1 teaspoon Edmonds baking
powder
1 teaspoon ground ginger

GINGER ICING
75 g butter
3/4 cup icing sugar
2 tablespoons golden syrup
3 teaspoons ground ginger

Cream butter and sugar until light and fluffy. Sift flour, baking powder and ginger together. Mix into creamed mixture. Turn dough out onto a lightly floured board. Knead well. Press dough into a greased 20 x 30 cm sponge roll tin. Bake at 190ºC for 20–25 minutes or until golden.

Pour hot Ginger Icing over base while hot and cut into 5-cm squares while still warm. To make the Ginger Icing, combine butter, icing sugar, golden syrup and ginger in a small saucepan. Heat until butter is melted, stirring constantly. **MAKES 24**

peanut **brownies**

125 g butter, softened
1 cup sugar
1 egg
1½ cups Edmonds standard grade
   flour

1 teaspoon Edmonds baking
   powder
pinch of salt
2 tablespoons cocoa
1 cup blanched peanuts, roasted

~ Cream butter and sugar until light and fluffy. Add egg and beat well. Sift flour, baking powder, salt and cocoa together. Mix into creamed mixture. Add cold peanuts and mix well.

    Roll tablespoons of mixture into balls. Place on greased oven trays. Flatten with a floured fork. Bake at 180ºC for 15 minutes or until cooked.   **MAKES 35**

---

american chocolate **brownies**

175 g butter
250 g cooking chocolate, chopped
1½ cups Edmonds standard
   grade flour
1 cup sugar

2 teaspoons vanilla essence
3 eggs, beaten
icing sugar to dust
Chocolate Icing (see page 134)
1 cup walnuts, chopped (optional)

~ In a medium-sized saucepan, melt butter and chocolate over a low heat. Remove saucepan from the heat and add flour, sugar, vanilla and eggs. Stir until well combined. Pour mixture into a 20-cm square tin lined on the base with baking paper.

    Bake at 180ºC for 40 minutes. Leave in tin for 10 minutes before turning out onto a wire rack. When cold, dust with icing sugar, or ice with Chocolate Icing and top with chopped walnuts. Cut into 4-cm squares.   **MAKES 25 SQUARES**

---

brownie point

Measure out the slice with a ruler to get even pieces of brownie.

afghans

200 g butter, softened
1/2 cup sugar
1 1/4 cups Edmonds standard
    grade flour

1/4 cup cocoa
2 cups cornflakes

Cream butter and sugar until light and fluffy. Sift flour and cocoa. Stir into creamed mixture. Fold in cornflakes. Spoon mounds of mixture onto a greased oven tray, gently pressing the mixture together. Bake at 180ºC for 15 minutes or until set. When cold ice with Chocolate Icing (see page 134). **MAKES 30**

Variation
afghan slice
Press afghan mixture into a 20 x 30 cm sponge roll tin. Bake at 180ºC for 25 minutes or until set. When cold, ice with Chocolate Icing.

---

ginger biscuits

200 g butter, softened
3/4 cup caster sugar
1/4 cup golden syrup
2 1/4 cups Edmonds standard
    grade flour

2 teaspoons Edmonds baking soda
1 tablespoon ground ginger

Cream butter and caster sugar until light and fluffy. Add golden syrup and beat well. Sift dry ingredients. Stir into creamed mixture to form a soft dough.

Roll heaped teaspoons of mixture into balls. Place balls 3–4 cm apart on greased oven trays. Flatten biscuits slightly with the palm of your hand. Bake at 160ºC for 30 minutes. Cool on wire racks. **MAKES 38 BISCUITS**

paper chase

If making a large batch of biscuits, place spoonfuls of mixture onto sheets of baking paper the same size as your oven trays. This way they can be easily transferred to the oven tray before and after cooking.

mud cake

BASE
200 g packet chocolate thin biscuits
75 g butter
1/2 cup chocolate hazelnut spread

CAKE
50 g butter
1 cup sugar
3 eggs
1 tablespoon vanilla essence

1 1/2 cups Edmonds standard grade
  flour
3 teaspoons Edmonds baking
  powder
3 tablespoons cocoa
1/4 cup boiling water
1/2 cup milk
icing sugar to dust
ready-made chocolate sauce

To make the base, crush biscuits into fine crumbs. Melt butter and mix into biscuit crumbs. Press over the base of a 20-cm round cake tin lined on the base with baking paper. Spread with hazelnut spread.

To make the cake, melt butter in a saucepan large enough to mix all the ingredients. Remove from heat. Add sugar, eggs and vanilla. Sift flour and baking powder together. Mix cocoa into boiling water. Fold flour, cocoa mixture and milk into butter mixture. Pour over base.

Bake at 180ºC for 45–50 minutes, or until cake springs back when lightly touched. Cool in tin for 10 minutes before turning onto a wire rack.

Dust with icing sugar and serve with chocolate sauce.

sultana cake

2 cups sultanas
250 g butter, chopped in small
  pieces
2 cups sugar
3 eggs, beaten
1/2 teaspoon lemon essence or
  almond essence

3 cups Edmonds standard grade
  flour
1 1/2 teaspoons Edmonds baking
  powder

Put sultanas in a saucepan. Cover with water. Bring to the boil, then simmer for 15 minutes. Drain thoroughly. Add butter.

In a bowl, beat sugar into eggs until well combined. Add sultana mixture and essence. Sift flour and baking powder together. Mix sifted ingredients into fruit mixture. Spoon mixture into a greased and lined 20-cm square cake tin.

Bake at 160ºC for 1–1 1/2 hours or until cake springs back when lightly touched. Leave in tin for 10 minutes before turning onto a wire rack.

cakes and
baking

chocolate cake

175 g butter, softened
1 teaspoon vanilla essence
1³/₄ cups sugar
3 eggs
2 cups Edmonds standard grade
    flour

¹/₂ cup cocoa
2 teaspoons Edmonds baking
    powder
1 cup milk
Chocolate Icing (see page 134) or
    icing sugar

Cream butter, essence and sugar until light and fluffy. Add eggs one at a time, beating well after each addition. Sift together flour, cocoa and baking powder. Fold into creamed mixture alternately with milk.

Spoon mixture into a greased and lined 22-cm round cake tin. Bake at 180ºC for 55–60 minutes or until a skewer inserted in the centre comes out clean. Leave in tin for 10 minutes before turning out onto a wire rack.

When cold, ice with Chocolate Icing or dust with icing sugar.

coffee cake

250 g butter, softened
1¹/₂ cups caster sugar
3 eggs
2 cups Edmonds standard grade
    flour
2 teaspoons Edmonds baking
    powder

2 tablespoons coffee and chicory
    essence
³/₄ cup milk
Coffee Icing (see page 134)

Cream butter and sugar until light and fluffy. Add eggs one at a time, beating well after each addition. Sift together flour and baking powder. Combine essence and milk. Fold dry ingredients and milk alternately into creamed mixture.

Spoon into a deep 22-cm round cake tin after you have lined the base with baking paper. Bake at 180ºC for 50–55 minutes or until a skewer inserted in the centre of the cake comes out clean. Leave cake in tin for 10 minutes before turning onto a wire rack. When cold, spread with Coffee Icing.

carrot cake

3 eggs
1 cup sugar
3/4 cup vegetable oil
2 cups Edmonds standard grade
   flour
1 teaspoon Edmonds baking
   powder
1 teaspoon Edmonds baking soda
1/2 teaspoon cinnamon

3 cups grated carrots
3/4 cup (225 g can) drained
   unsweetened crushed pineapple
1/2 cup chopped walnuts
1 teaspoon grated orange rind
   (optional)
Cream Cheese Icing (see page 134)
orange zest to garnish

Beat together eggs and sugar for 5 minutes until thick. Add oil and beat for 1 minute. Sift flour, baking powder, baking soda and cinnamon.

Combine carrot, pineapple, walnuts and orange rind. Fold into egg mixture. Fold in dry ingredients. Grease a deep 20-cm ring tin. Line base with baking paper. Spoon mixture into tin.

Bake at 180ºC for 50–55 minutes or until a skewer inserted in the centre of the cake comes out clean. Leave in tin for 10 minutes before turning out onto a wire rack. When cold, spread with Cream Cheese Icing and garnish with orange zest.

banana cake

125 g butter, softened
3/4 cup sugar
2 eggs
1 1/2 cups mashed ripe bananas
   (about 4 medium bananas)
1 teaspoon Edmonds baking soda
2 tablespoons hot milk

2 cups Edmonds standard
   grade flour
1 teaspoon Edmonds baking
   powder
Lemon Icing (see page 134)
lemon zest to garnish

Cream butter and sugar until light and fluffy. Add eggs one at a time, beating well after each addition. Add mashed banana and mix thoroughly. Stir soda into hot milk and add to creamed mixture. Sift flour and baking powder. Fold into mixture. Turn into a greased and lined 20-cm round cake tin.

Bake at 180ºC for 50 minutes or until cake springs back when lightly touched. Leave in tin for 10 minutes before turning out onto a wire rack. When cold, ice with Lemon Icing and garnish with lemon zest.

Variation
The mixture can be baked in two 20-cm round sandwich tins at 180ºC for 25 minutes. The two cakes can be filled with whipped cream and sliced banana.

pastry and icings

short pastry

2 cups Edmonds standard grade
   flour
1/4 teaspoon salt
125 g butter
cold water

Sift flour and salt together. Cut in the butter until mixture resembles fine breadcrumbs. Mix to a stiff dough with a little water. Roll out very lightly and do not handle more than is necessary. Use as required for sweet or savoury pies and tarts, and quiches. Makes 375 g pastry.

sweet short pastry

1 cup Edmonds standard grade
   flour
75 g butter
1/4 cup sugar
1 egg yolk
1 tablespoon water

To make pastry, sift flour. Cut butter into flour until mixture resembles fine breadcrumbs. Stir in sugar. Add yolk and water. Mix to a stiff dough. Cover with plastic wrap and chill for 30 minutes before using. Makes about 200 g pastry.

cream cheese icing

2 tablespoons butter, softened
1/4 cup cream cheese
1 cup icing sugar
1/2 teaspoon grated lemon rind

Beat butter and cream cheese until creamy. Mix in icing sugar and lemon rind, beating well to combine.

white icing

2 cups icing sugar
1/4 cup butter, softened
2 tablespoons (approximately)
   water
1/2 teaspoon vanilla essence

Sift icing sugar into a bowl. Add butter. Add sufficient water to mix to a spreadable consistency. Flavour with essence.

chocolate icing

2 cups icing sugar
2 tablespoons cocoa
1/4 cup butter
1/4 teaspoon vanilla essence
2 tablespoons boiling water
walnuts (optional)

Sift icing sugar and cocoa into a bowl. Add butter and essence. Add sufficient boiling water to mix to a spreadable consistency. Decorate with a walnut if desired.

coffee icing

Dissolve 2 teaspoons instant coffee in 1 tablespoon hot water. Mix into White Icing recipe.

lemon icing

Replace vanilla in White Icing recipe with 1 teaspoon grated lemon rind. Replace water with lemon juice. Add a few drops of yellow food colouring if desired.

a christmas feast

It happens every year and all the fuss usually culminates in a wonderful meal and a severe bloated feeling afterwards! The trick to coping with Christmas is being organised. Planning and time management will help ease every strain, from preparing a meal to shopping for presents and Christmas goodies.

Plan to get your Christmas turkey and ham early. Allow for the freezer space and remember to thaw the bird well in advance. If cooking a ham, check whether it needs to be soaked or whether other preparations should be made. Buying a pre-cooked ham saves a lot of work.

If you are looking for a vegetarian alternative, try the Greek dish, Spanakopita (see page 137). Make the dish at least once before Christmas to test the method and see if you like it. There is nothing worse than a failure when your nearest and dearest are sitting around a table ready for the big dinner.

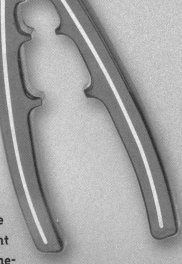

Think of simple ways to make Christmas extra-special. Try setting a table in one colour theme — masses of gold or silver — or place a little gift on the starter or dessert plate for each guest.

On a budget, Christmas can be overwhelming. If you are entertaining a group of good friends, suggest a pot-luck Christmas dinner. With some subtle planning, each guest can bring a different dish and so eliminate excessive cost and time-consuming preparations.

glazed ham

4–5 kg ham
2 tablespoons wholegrain mustard
1 teaspoon ground cloves
1 teaspoon nutmeg

4 tablespoons brown sugar
4 tablespoons liquid honey
2 tablespoons orange juice
thin slices of orange

Soak the ham if it requires it, but check to see what it says on the pack. With a sharp knife, loosen edges of skin, then peel it away. Trim excess fat, if any, but leave at least an 8-mm thickness. Score fat into a diamond pattern. Try not to cut too deeply as cuts will open further during cooking.

Mix mustard, spices, sugar and honey with enough orange juice to make a paste that will spread. Smooth this all over the fat surface. Bake ham at 200ºC for 15 minutes or more until nicely golden.   **SERVES 6–8**

roast turkey

4.5–5.5 kg turkey (thawed if it
    was frozen)
50 g butter, at room temperature
sage and parsley sprigs, to garnish

STUFFING
1 onion, finely chopped

8 rashers streaky bacon, diced
250 g fresh white breadcrumbs
350 g sausage meat
2 tablespoons mixed herbs
juice of 1 lemon
2 eggs

Preheat the oven to 190ºC. Remove the giblets from the turkey and wash the bird inside and out. Dry well with kitchen paper.

To prepare the stuffing, sauté the onions and bacon together for 5 minutes until onion is softened. Mix bacon and onion with all remaining ingredients in a large bowl. Spoon stuffing into cavity. Close the cavity using a wooden skewer. Cross legs of turkey and tie together with string for a good shape.

Grease a large roasting pan with a little butter. Smear the rest over the turkey skin and season well, then put in the tin. Loosely cover with foil and roast. A turkey should be roasted at 18 minutes per 450 g plus 25 minutes finishing time.

Baste turkey every hour. One hour before the end of cooking remove the foil and drain off excess fat. To test whether the turkey is cooked, insert a skewer into the thickest part of the thigh — the juices should run clear. If they are pinkish, cook for 15 minutes more, then test again. Serve on a large platter garnished with vegetables, stuffing, sage and parsley.   **SERVES 10–12**

mini sausages with bacon

24 mini sausages or saveloys   **12 rashers streaky bacon**

 Cut the rashers of bacon in half, widthways. Wrap each sausage in a piece of bacon, tucking the ends underneath. Place the sausages in a roasting tray and bake in oven at 180ºC for 15 minutes, until bacon is crispy and sausages are cooked. Serve arranged around the Christmas turkey.   **MAKES 24**

Tip: Spicy sausages such as small chorizo are also perfect for this recipe.

---

spanakopita

115 g butter, melted
900 g frozen spinach, thawed
400 g feta, crumbled
2 tablespoons freshly grated
**   parmesan cheese**
6 spring onions, finely sliced

1/4 cup fresh dill
4 eggs, beaten
1/2 teaspoon ground nutmeg
freshly ground black pepper
275 g Edmonds filo pastry (about
**   12 sheets)**

 Grease a 19 x 27 cm roasting pan with some of the melted butter. Drain the spinach in a colander, gently squeezing out as much excess water as you can.

Place the spinach, feta and parmesan cheeses, spring onions, dill, eggs and nutmeg in a large bowl; season with black pepper and mix well.

Brush one side of each sheet of filo with melted butter. Layer 10 of the filo sheets butter-side down in the tin, leaving a generous quantity hanging over the edges.

Spoon the spinach mixture into the tin and fold the overhanging filo pastry edges over the filling. Brush the pastry with a little more butter. Place the last two sheets of filo on top of the pie and tuck the edges down the sides. Brush with butter and cut the top layer of the pastry into squares or wedges. Bake in oven at 180ºC for 1 1/4 hours, then allow to stand for 10 minutes to set.

SERVES 8

---

a christmas
feast

pavlova

4 egg whites
1 1/2 cups caster sugar
1 teaspoon white vinegar
1 teaspoon vanilla essence

1 tablespoon Edmonds Fielder's
  cornflour
whipped cream
fresh berries and mint leaves
  to garnish

∾ Preheat oven to 180ºC. Using an electric mixer, beat egg whites and caster sugar for 10–15 minutes or until thick and glossy. Mix vinegar, vanilla essence and cornflour together. Add to meringue. Beat on high speed for a further 5 minutes.

Line an oven tray with baking paper. Draw a 22-cm circle on the baking paper. Spread the pavlova to within 2 cm of the edge of the circle, keeping the shape as round and even as possible. Smooth top surface. Place pavlova in preheated oven then turn oven temperature down to 100ºC. Bake pavlova for 1 hour. Turn off oven. Open oven door slightly and leave pavlova in oven until cold. Carefully lift pavlova onto a serving plate. Decorate with whipped cream, fresh berries and mint leaves.

SERVES 6

sherry trifle

1/4 cup Edmonds custard powder
3 tablespoons sugar
2 cups milk
2 egg whites
200 g trifle sponge
1/4 cup raspberry or apricot jam

1/4 cup sherry
410 g can fruit salad
3/4 cup cream
2 teaspoons icing sugar
1/4 cup toasted slivered almonds to
  decorate

∾ To make the custard, mix custard powder, sugar and 1/4 cup of the milk to a smooth paste in a saucepan. Add remaining milk and stir over a low heat until mixture comes to the boil. Simmer for 2–3 minutes or until custard thickens, stirring constantly. Remove from heat, cover and leave until cold. When custard has cooled, beat egg whites until stiff. Fold custard into egg whites.

Cut sponge in half horizontally. Spread cut surface with jam. Sandwich halves together. Cut into cubes then arrange in 6 individual serving dishes or 1 large serving bowl. Spoon sherry over sponge. Spoon fruit salad and juice evenly over sponge. Spoon custard over fruit salad.

Chill until set. Beat cream and icing sugar until thick. Decorate trifle with cream and almonds.

SERVES 6

party food

Food is a good start at a drinks party or any social gathering! Small nibbles can line the stomach and keep rumbling tums at bay. The food can also be matched well with the wine, or other beverages being offered.

You don't want to be fussing about in the kitchen with elaborate party food before your big event of the year. Keep your preparations simple. Choose a theme such as Japanese, Mexican or Middle Eastern, and serve goodies from those countries. It's also a good idea to serve wines and beverages from that country as well.

Choose from a selection of recipes or make simple put-togethers like kiwifruit wrapped in ham or nacho chips with a little guacamole spooned on top. Wrap salami around olives or spread blue cheese on oat crackers.

Parties are a good time to serve antipasto platters or cheeseboards (see page 46). Or serve tapenades (see page 61) and cream cheese spreads (see pages 45 and 142).

Always take into consideration how many guests are coming and what their tastes are. Some crowds might not appreciate dainty food and might need something more substantial. Others may prefer delicacies.

At the end of the day, you want to enjoy your own party — so keep it simple and manageable.

crostini with toppings

2 cloves garlic
1/4 cup olive oil
1 loaf French bread

TOPPINGS
hummus (see page 45)
roasted red capsicums, cut
    into strips

Parma ham
cherry tomatoes
pesto
tapenade (see page 61)
sour cream

Crush, peel and mash garlic. Mix with oil. Cut bread into 1-cm slices. Brush bread liberally with garlic-flavoured oil. Place on a baking tray and bake at 190ºC for 10 minutes. Turn and cook other side for 2–3 minutes. Leave until cold. Can be stored in an airtight container.

To serve, spoon a mixture of the above toppings onto each crostini and season well with freshly ground black pepper.   **MAKES ABOUT 60**

cheese ball

250 g cream cheese
1 cup grated tasty cheddar cheese
1 pickled onion, finely chopped
2 tablespoons finely chopped
    parsley
2 tablespoons finely chopped
    gherkin
1 tablespoon tomato sauce

1 teaspoon Worcestershire sauce
few drops Tabasco sauce
1/4 teaspoon paprika
1/2 cup (approximately) chopped
    walnuts
crackers or sliced fresh bread
    to serve

Combine cheeses in a bowl. Add pickled onion, parsley, gherkin, tomato, Worcestershire and Tabasco sauces and paprika. Beat well to combine. Shape into a ball. Roll in chopped walnuts until well coated. Wrap and chill until firm. Serve with crackers or sliced fresh bread.   **MAKES 1 1/2 CUPS**

savoury pita bread

large pita bread
butter, softened
garlic, crushed

grated cheese
sesame seeds or poppy seeds

ᴖ Cut the pita bread in half horizontally. Spread the split side with butter and garlic. Top with cheese and sesame seeds. Cut into wedges.

Place on an oven tray. Cook at 190ºC for 10 minutes or until golden. Serve hot or cold. Serve with an antipasto platter or cheeseboard (page 46).

---

savoury mini-pinwheel scones

SCONE DOUGH
3 cups Edmonds standard grade
   flour
6 teaspoons Edmonds baking
   powder
1/4 teaspoon salt
75 g butter
1–11/2 (approximately) cups milk

extra milk

TOPPINGS
1/4 cup pesto
1/4 cup sundried-tomato tapenade
1/4 cup olive tapenade
1 egg, beaten

ᴖ Sift flour, baking powder and salt into a bowl. Cut butter in until mixture resembles fine breadcrumbs. Add milk and mix quickly with a knife to a soft dough. Knead a few times. Roll out the dough on a floured board to 0.5-cm thickness. Cut into three sections.

Spread each section with one of the toppings. Roll up the pieces of dough, from the long side. Slice each log into about 12 small sections. Lightly dust an oven tray with flour.

Place each slice on the tray and brush with the beaten egg. Bake at 220ºC for 10 minutes or until golden brown. **MAKES 36**

---

blue cheese spread

250 g blue cheese
150 g cream cheese
1 small onion, chopped
2 tablespoons softened butter
1 tablespoon Worcestershire sauce

dash Tabasco sauce
2 tablespoons dry sherry
pumpernickel bread and crostini,
   to serve
tiny sprigs of fresh herbs to garnish

⚬ Crumble blue cheese into the bowl of a food processor. Add cream cheese, onion, butter, Worcestershire and Tabasco sauces, and sherry.

Process until smooth. Transfer to a bowl. Cover and refrigerate until firm. When ready to use, spread on pumpernickel bread or crostini. Garnish with sprigs of fresh herbs.

MAKES 1½ CUPS

corn and tomato salsa

1 onion, finely chopped
2 cloves garlic, crushed
450 g can whole peeled tomatoes,
   roughly chopped
½ cup whole corn kernels
½ green capsicum, deseeded and
   finely chopped
1 teaspoon cumin

1 teaspoon basil
½ teaspoon rosemary
½ teaspoon paprika
¼ teaspoon chilli
1 tablespoon chives, finely chopped
½ teaspoon salt

⚬ Combine all ingredients in a saucepan and simmer for 5 minutes. Serve warm or cold with corn chips.

MAKES ABOUT 2 CUPS

devilled eggs

12 eggs, hard-boiled
⅔ cup cream cheese
⅔ cup finely shredded smoked
   cheddar cheese
1 teaspoon lemon juice
¼ teaspoon salt

¼ teaspoon ground cumin
⅛ teaspoon cayenne pepper
freshly ground black pepper

⚬ Shell eggs. Cut in half. Remove yolks and place them in a medium-sized bowl. Mash well. Add remaining ingredients, except black pepper. Beat until fluffy.

Using a pastry bag, pipe mixture back into egg whites. Cover and chill. Season to taste with black pepper before serving.

MAKES 24

sushi

2 cups short grain rice
3 cups cold water
1/3 cup sugar
1/3 cup rice vinegar
1 level tablespoon salt
7 toasted nori sheets
2 teaspoons wasabi paste

FILLING COMBINATIONS
(all finely sliced into strips)
- pickled ginger, telegraph cucumber and red capsicum
- smoked salmon, telegraph cucumber and yellow capsicum
- carrot, telegraph cucumber and red capsicum
- smoked chicken, telegraph cucumber, and red capsicum

TO SERVE
3 tablespoons light soy sauce
1 teaspoon wasabi paste
pickled ginger

Place rice in a sieve. Rinse thoroughly under cold running water. Place rice and water in a saucepan. Set aside for 30 minutes. Cover pan and bring to the boil over a high heat. Reduce heat to very low and simmer for about 15 minutes, that is, until all the water has been absorbed. Turn off heat and let stand for 15 minutes. Combine sugar, vinegar and salt. Gradually add to the rice, tossing rice with a fork. Cover and set aside for 10 minutes to cool slightly.

Divide rice into 7 equal portions. To assemble, place a sheet of nori, rough side up, on a damp bamboo sushi mat. Spread one portion of rice over the nori. Using the wasabi paste sparingly, spread a narrow line across one end of the rice, 2.5 cm from the edge. Arrange filling ingredients of choice along the line of wasabi.

Starting at the edge with the filling, use the bamboo mat to help you roll the sushi into a tight log, pressing down firmly as you roll. Using a sharp knife, trim off ends, and then cut log into 5 equal portions. Transfer to a serving dish. Serve with soy sauce, wasabi paste and pickled ginger. **MAKES 35 PIECES**

mini herb and feta fritters

1/2 cup Edmonds standard grade
    flour
1/2 teaspoon salt
1/2 teaspoon curry powder
1/2 teaspoon Edmonds baking
    powder
1/4 cup grated onion

1/2 cup milk
1/2 cup crumbled feta cheese
1/4 cup finely chopped fresh herbs,
    such as parsley, sage, mint,
    and coriander
1 egg white
2 tablespoons oil

Sift flour, salt, curry powder and baking powder into a bowl. Stir in onion. Gradually add milk, mixing until smooth. Batter should be the consistency of thick cream. Stir in the feta cheese and herbs.

In another bowl, beat the egg white until stiff but not dry. Carefully fold egg white into mixture. Heat oil in a frying pan. Drop teaspoonfuls of mixture into pan. Cook until golden, then turn and cook other side. Drain on absorbent paper. Serve hot.

MAKES 40

potato pancakes
with smoked salmon

POTATO PANCAKES
1 cup Edmonds standard grade
    flour
1/4 teaspoon salt
1 egg
1 cup milk
1 cup mashed potato
water

FILLING
250 g pot crème fraîche
sprigs of dill, plus extra for
    garnishing
450 g smoked salmon slices

To make the pancakes: Sift flour and salt into a bowl. Add egg, mixing to combine. Gradually beat in milk and potato, mixing to a smooth batter. Chill for 1 hour. Stir. The batter will thicken on standing. Add a little water if necessary to bring it back to the original consistency.

Heat a greased pancake pan or small frying pan. Cook teaspoonfuls of the mixture until golden on underside, then turn. Drain on kitchen paper.
To assemble: Finely chop some of the dill sprigs. Mix dill into the crème fraîche. Place teaspoonfuls of the crème mixture on each potato pancake. Top with a small piece of smoked salmon. Garnish with small pieces of dill.
MAKES 36

savoury **tartlets**

2 rashers bacon, chopped
1 onion, finely chopped
2 eggs
1 cup milk
salt and freshly ground
   black pepper

400 g packet Edmonds flaky pastry
1 tablespoon (approximately)
   chopped parsley

Cook bacon and onion in a frying pan until onion is clear. Set aside to cool. In a bowl, combine eggs, milk and salt and pepper to taste.

On a lightly floured board, roll out pastry to 6-mm thickness. Cut out rounds and use to line patty tins. Spoon a little of the onion mixture into each pastry case. Top with parsley.

Spoon egg mixture over. Bake at 200ºC for 15 minutes or until golden and set. Serve hot.

MAKES ABOUT 24

party partners

If serving wine and other drinks with your party food try to match the food with the flavour of the wine. As a general rule, strongly flavoured food such as blue cheese will go with robust reds, while lighter flavours such as salmon will match crisper wines such as sauvignon blanc.

let's party

- It is called 'finger food' because guests should be able to pick it up with their fingers, and pop it into their mouths in one go. A party is no time for cutlery or large mouthfuls. Keep the selection of food to bite-sized pieces.

- Serve your food in stages — hot and cold snacks can be served alternately over a period of an hour, instead of serving them all at once.

- Accompany your snacks with serviettes, so that guests can clean up messy fingers. Have plenty of places where guests can dispose of empty plates or napkins.

- Serve your snacks creatively — use wooden cutting boards, mirrors, plain glass or unusual platters.

- Keep the hot food hot and the cold food cold. There's nothing worse than lukewarm food.

- Match your food to the wine and drinks you are serving.

- Prepare as much as you can ahead of time.

- Consider quick and easy garnishes to decorate your food on the serving platters.

dinner for two

Maybe you're planning a romantic dinner or perhaps you just want to impress someone special. Cooking for two is always a pleasure, even if it's only because you deserve to cook something a little special every now and then.

By refining your recipes and paying a little more attention to your cooking, you can create your own 'signature' dishes that you will be remembered for.

In a romantic sense it is not just the food that does the talking. Set the scene with candles and fine music. And pay attention to the details, such as serving a good wine, having matching table settings and creating an ambience.

That is not to say you have to confine your eating to the dining room. Try setting up a picnic or a special meal somewhere romantic, like a beach or in a park.

Prepare well in advance so that you don't meet your guest in an apron at the door.

Try a theme such as Asian, Mediterranean, seafood or vegetarian (see the suggested menus on page 148), or match your dishes to a selection of wines for extra-special enjoyment.

dinner for two
menu suggestions

Menu 1
Romantic
Asparagus with Parma Ham
(see opposite)
Baked Fish with Crumb Topping served with fresh salad
(see page 151)
Chocolate Cream Pots
(see page 155)

Menu 2
Special
Sushi
(see page 143)
Salmon Fillets with Teriyaki Sauce
(see page 150)
Meringue and Raspberry Cream
(see page 156)

Menu 3
Vegetarian
Mini Herb and Feta Fritters
(see page 144)
Eggplant and Tomato Pie
(see page 108)
Banoffee Pie
(see page 122)

Menu 4
Picnic
Blue Cheese Spread with Crostini
(see pages 142 and 140)
Cajun Spiced Chicken and Marinated Chicken Wings
(see pages 153 and 79)
Fruit Kebabs
(see page 115)

asparagus with parma ham

10 asparagus spears
10 slices Parma ham or prosciutto
unsalted butter, melted

salt and freshly ground
   black pepper

Trim and peel the asparagus spears. Bring a pot of water to the boil. Drop the spears in a few at a time, then drain and refresh in cold water.

Wrap a piece of ham or prosciutto around each piece of asparagus. Brush with melted butter and season with salt and pepper. Cook under a preheated grill, turning once, for about 3 minutes.   SERVES 2

creamy gnocchi

450 g pre-made potato gnocchi
1 tablespoon olive oil
1 onion, finely sliced
2 spring onions, finely sliced
1 tablespoon fresh, chopped
   parsley

1 tablespoon fresh, chopped sage
250 g crème fraîche
salt and freshly ground
   black pepper
$1/2$ cup toasted pinenuts

Cook gnocchi according to instructions on packet. Drain well. In a frying pan, heat the oil. Fry onion and spring onions until softened. Add parsley and sage and cook for 2–3 minutes.

Stir in crème fraîche and cook for 5 minutes, until mixture is just beginning to bubble. Remove from heat and stir in gnocchi. Season to taste. Sprinkle toasted pinenuts on top. Serve immediately.   SERVES 2

thai prawn salad

85 g rice noodles
2 tablespoons olive oil
1 clove garlic, finely sliced
salt and freshly ground
    black pepper
1 red chilli, finely sliced
2 teaspoons root ginger,
    finely sliced

12 tiger prawns
140 g green beans, halved
2 tablespoons sweet chilli sauce
juice of 2 limes
1 teaspoon sugar
a handful of chopped fresh
    coriander
lime wedges, to serve

Put noodles in a large bowl. Cover with boiling water. Set aside for 4 minutes. Drain, and then refresh under cold running water.

Mix oil, garlic, salt, pepper, half the chilli and 1 teaspoon of the ginger together. Pour over prawns. Heat large frying pan and fry prawns for 2 minutes, turning once.

Cook green beans in boiling, salted water for 3 minutes until tender. Drain, then plunge into cold water to stop the cooking process. Mix together chilli sauce, lime juice, sugar, remaining ginger and chilli, and most of the coriander.

Mix prawns, beans and noodles. Toss with chilli dressing. Spoon into serving bowls. Garnish with remaining coriander and serve with lime wedges.

SERVES 2

salmon fillets
with teriyaki sauce

2 x 200 g salmon fillets, trimmed
    and bones removed
3 tablespoons soy sauce
2 tablespoons tomato sauce
1 teaspoon sambal oelek
1 tablespoon brown sugar

2 cloves garlic, finely chopped
juice of 1 lemon
2 tablespoons oil
new potatoes and steamed
    broccoli, to serve
lemon wedges to garnish

Lay the salmon fillets flat in a tray. In a bowl, mix together the soy sauce, tomato sauce, sambal oelek, brown sugar, garlic and lemon juice. Pour the teriyaki sauce over the fish. Leave to marinate for 30 minutes.

In a frying pan, heat the oil. Cook the salmon fillets for 2–3 minutes each side, until the flesh has just turned opaque. Leave to rest for 5 minutes before serving.

SERVES 2

baked fish
with crumb topping

85 g fresh breadcrumbs (2 thick
   slices of bread)
2 tablespoons olive oil
1 courgette, finely grated
2 tablespoons fresh parsley,
   chopped

50 g freshly grated
   parmesan cheese
zest of 1 lemon
salt and freshly ground black pepper
2 boneless white fish fillets, e.g.
   tarakihi, hapuka or snapper

❧ Mix together the breadcrumbs, olive oil, courgette, parsley, parmesan and lemon zest, then season.

Put the fish fillets on a baking tray lined with lightly greased foil. Press the crumbs firmly onto each fillet so they stick. Bake at 180ºC for 15–20 minutes until the fish is just cooked and the topping is golden. Serve with asparagus spears and new potatoes. **SERVES 2**

scallops mornay

1 dozen scallops
1 tablespoon butter
1 tablespoon Edmonds standard
   grade flour
³/₄ cup milk
¹/₄ cup grated tasty cheddar cheese

salt and freshly ground
   black pepper
1 cup hot mashed potato

❧ Remove any feed tubes from scallops. Set scallops aside. Melt butter in a saucepan. Stir in flour and cook until frothy. Gradually add milk, stirring constantly until mixture boils. Add scallops to sauce. Continue cooking for 5 minutes, stirring occasionally.

Remove from heat and stir in half the cheese. Season with salt and pepper to taste. Decorate edge of scallop shells or ovenproof dish with mashed potato. Spoon scallop mixture into serving shells or dish to be used. Sprinkle remaining cheese on top. Grill until golden. **SERVES 2**

chorizo and sage **risotto**

3 tablespoons olive oil
85 g butter
1 large onion, finely chopped
1 tablespoon fresh sage leaves,
    chopped, plus extra for garnish

450 g chorizo sausages, cut into
    1-cm pieces
350 g arborio rice
3/4 cup red wine
5 cups hot vegetable stock
50 g freshly grated parmesan cheese

Heat the oil and half the butter in a large pan and cook the onion and sage for 2 minutes. Add the chorizo pieces and cook for 3–4 minutes until starting to brown.

Add the rice and cook for 5–7 minutes, stirring, until slightly translucent.

Add the wine and cook over a moderate heat, stirring all the time, adding ladlefuls of stock to keep the consistency soupy, for 15 minutes. Add the remaining butter, cut into small pieces, and most of the parmesan.

Season and allow to stand for 1 minute before serving. Top with sage leaves, remaining parmesan and freshly ground black pepper.   **SERVES 2–4**

rack of lamb **with spicy chickpeas**

1 tablespoon coriander seeds
1 teaspoon crushed chilli flakes
2 teaspoons olive oil
1/4 teaspoon salt
1 garlic clove, finely chopped
1 teaspoon mustard seeds
1 tablespoon chopped fresh
    coriander
1 rack of lamb with 6 ribs

2 tablespoons red wine
1/2 teaspoon Dijon mustard

SPICY CHICKPEAS
1 small onion, sliced into rings
2 tablespoons olive oil
1 garlic clove, finely chopped
good pinch dried chilli flakes
400 g can chickpeas, drained
big handful of baby spinach leaves

Preheat the oven to 220°C. Dry-fry the coriander seeds in a frying pan on a medium heat until toasted. Remove from the pan, crush and mix with the chilli flakes, oil, salt, garlic, mustard seeds and fresh coriander.

Put the meat in a roasting pan. Spread with the mixture. Roast for 20 minutes.

Fry the onion in oil on a high heat until golden. Add the garlic, chilli and, after a minute, the chickpeas. Set aside.

Remove the lamb, loosely cover with foil, and allow to rest for 5–10 minutes. Add the spinach to the chickpeas and cook, stirring for 30 seconds. Add any meat juices to the gravy and reheat. Halve the rack. Cut through each cutlet but don't separate. Serve opened out on the chickpeas; drizzle with gravy.   **SERVES 2**

cajun spiced chicken

2 chicken breasts, skin removed
2 tablespoons melted butter
1/4 cup flour
2 tablespoons Cajun spice mix

1/4 teaspoon cayenne pepper
  (optional)
salt and freshly ground
  black pepper

Trim the chicken breasts and pat dry with kitchen paper. Brush over the melted butter to coat whole of each breast. Mix together the flour, Cajun spice mix, cayenne pepper (optional) and season to taste.

Lay the breasts on an oven tray. Cook in oven at 180ºC for 20–25 minutes, until golden brown, turning once. Serve with Spinach Salad (see page 54).

SERVES 2

---

lemon chicken

3 lemons
50 g butter
3 tablespoons liquid honey
1 clove garlic, chopped
4 rosemary sprigs, leaves stripped
  from the stalks

salt and freshly ground black
  pepper
6 chicken drumsticks
400 g potatoes, cut into small
  chunks
green salad, to serve

Put the juice of 2 of the lemons, butter, honey, garlic and rosemary in a small pan. Season to taste with salt and pepper. Heat gently until butter melts.

Arrange chicken pieces in 1 layer in a shallow roasting pan. Put the potatoes around the chicken. Drizzle over the lemon butter, turning the potatoes until evenly coated. Cut the remaining lemon into eight wedges and add to roasting pan.

Place dish in oven at 200ºC for 50 minutes to 1 hour. Stir once or twice until the chicken is cooked and the potatoes are crisp and golden. Serve with green salad.

SERVES 2

summer spaghetti
with tomato and brie

200 g spaghetti
250 g courgettes
2 tablespoons olive oil
2 garlic cloves, thinly sliced
3 ripe tomatoes, roughly chopped

juice and finely grated zest
    of 1 lemon
70 g brie cheese, diced
salt and freshly ground
    black pepper

∿ Cook spaghetti in boiling, salted water for 10–12 minutes until tender, or according to packet instructions. Drain and keep warm.

While spaghetti is cooking, cut courgettes in half lengthways, then cut into slices. Heat oil in a large frying pan. Fry courgettes and garlic for 2 minutes until softened. Add tomatoes, lemon zest and about 3 tablespoons of pasta water (enough to make a sauce).

Cook sauce for 10 minutes until tomatoes begin to soften. Remove from heat and stir in brie cheese so it just starts to melt. Season to taste with salt, pepper and lemon juice. Add spaghetti to tomato sauce mixture and toss well. Divide between 2 bowls and serve. **SERVES 2**

roasted vegetables
with garlic aioli

1 eggplant, cut into strips
2 carrots, peeled and cut into strips
1 red capsicum, deseeded and cut
    into strips
150 g green beans
2 potatoes, peeled and thinly sliced
3 tablespoons olive oil
4 cloves garlic, peeled and left whole

AIOLI
2 egg yolks
1 teaspoon crushed garlic
1 tablespoon lemon juice
1 cup olive oil
salt and freshly ground
    black pepper

∿ Place vegetables in a large roasting pan and mix through oil and garlic. Bake in oven at 220ºC for 35–40 minutes until starting to brown and crisp. Remove from oven and allow to cool down. Pile onto serving plates or large platter. Spoon over aioli and serve.
To make Aioli: Place yolks, garlic and lemon juice in a food processor. Blend until smooth. With the motor running, gradually add oil, a little at a time. The mixture will thicken. (If the oil is added too quickly, the aioli will curdle.) Season to taste. **SERVES 2**

fudgy brownies

1¹/₄ cups Edmonds standard
   grade flour
1 teaspoon salt
200 g unsalted butter

150 g dark chocolate, coarsely
   chopped
2 cups sugar
1 teaspoon vanilla essence
4 eggs

Sift the flour and salt. Melt the butter and chocolate together in a medium saucepan over a low heat, stirring frequently and being careful that it does not burn. Add half of the sugar to the mixture and stir for 30 seconds, then remove the pan from the heat and stir in the essence. Pour the mixture into a large bowl.

In another bowl, beat together the remaining sugar and eggs until they are thick and creamy. Pour half of the sugar and egg mixture into the chocolate, stirring constantly.

Delicately fold in the remaining egg mixture. When the eggs are almost incorporated, gently fold in the dry ingredients. Pour the batter into a 20-cm square pan. Bake in oven at 160ºC for 35 minutes. When cold, cut into 4-cm squares and dust with icing sugar. **MAKES 25 SQUARES**

Tip: Lining your cake tins with baking paper makes the cake come out more easily and helps with cleaning.

chocolate cream pots

140 g dark chocolate
³/₄ cup cream
300 g mascarpone cheese

5 tablespoons Baileys Irish Cream
   liqueur
chocolate shavings, to decorate

Break chocolate into a bowl and microwave on High (100%) for 2–3 minutes or until melted. Stir and set aside.

Whisk cream to soft peaks. Whisk mascarpone cheese and Baileys together. Fold cream into mascarpone mixture. Pour in cooled chocolate (it should be the same temperature as cream mixture) and stir lightly to make a swirly pattern.

Spoon mixture into two 300 ml glasses. Cover generously with chocolate shavings and chill. **SERVES 2**

meringue and raspberry cream

MERINGUES
2 egg whites
$^{1}/_{2}$ cup caster sugar

RASPBERRY CREAM
$^{3}/_{4}$ cup cream
1 tablespoon icing sugar
200 g punnet raspberries
$^{1}/_{4}$ cup raspberry jam

To make meringues, beat egg whites until stiff but not dry. Add half the sugar and beat well. Repeat with remaining sugar. Pipe or spoon small amounts of meringue onto a greased oven tray. Bake at 120ºC for 1–1$^{1}/_{2}$ hours or until the meringues are dry but not brown.

Whip cream with icing sugar. Crumble 4 of the meringues into the cream. Mash half of the raspberries with a fork. Fold into the meringue-and-cream mixture. Leave to chill for 20 minutes. Arrange 4 meringues on 2 plates. Spoon the raspberry cream mixture over the top and add the remaining raspberries for decoration.

Mix the raspberry jam with 2 tablespoons of hot water. Drizzle a small amount over each dessert. Serve immediately.   **SERVES 2**

strawberry shortcakes

SHORTBREAD
125 g butter, softened
$^{1}/_{2}$ cup icing sugar
$^{1}/_{2}$ cup Edmonds Fielder's cornflour
1 cup Edmonds standard grade
    flour

FILLING
150 g mascarpone cheese
$^{1}/_{2}$ teaspoon vanilla essence
1 tablespoon icing sugar
rind of $^{1}/_{2}$ a lemon

150 g strawberries, hulled and
    sliced
icing sugar for dusting

To make the shortbread, cream butter and icing sugar until light and fluffy. Sift cornflour and flour together. Mix sifted ingredients into creamed mixture. Knead well. On a lightly floured board, roll out to 4–5-cm thickness. Shape into a circle or cut a circle using the edge of a teacup, about 5 cm in diameter. Place on a greased oven tray. Prick with a fork. Bake at 150ºC for 30 minutes or until pale golden. Allow to cool.

Mix together the filling ingredients — the mascarpone cheese, vanilla essence, icing sugar and lemon rind — until smooth. Spread some of the filling on one of the shortbread rounds. Top with some of the strawberry pieces. Place another shortbread on top and repeat. Top with a third biscuit. Dust with icing sugar and serve.

                                                    SERVES 2

chocolate cream pots
top and middle right
PAGE **155**

asparagus with parma ham
middle
PAGE **149**

baked fish with crumb topping
below
PAGE **151**

index

index